Brand Management in Commercial Banks:
A Study in Erode District of Tamilnadu

Dr.R. Shophiya,

Assistant Professor,

PG & Research Department of Commerce,

Gobi Arts & Science College (Autonomous),

Gobichettipalayam.

Published by

Brand Management in Commercial Banks: A Study in Erode District of Tamilnadu

ISBN 978-93-86638-99-1

Author

Dr.R. Shophiya

Bonfring

309, 2nd Floor,

5th Street Extension,

Gandhipuram,

Coimbatore-641 012.

Tamilnadu, India.

E-mail: info@bonfring.org

Website: www.bonfring.org

Phone: 0422 4213231

Preface

Commercial banks comprising public sector banks, private sector banks, regional rural banks, co-operative banks and foreign sector banks represent the most important financial intermediary in the Indian financial system. The Indian financial system is inherently strong, functionally diverse and displays efficiency and flexibility, critical to our national objectives of creating a market-driven, productive and competitive economy. Financial products and services brands offer a lot of benefits, for the customers as well as for the financial organisations. If a brand means association, than branding means recognition. The choice of brand elements includes choosing a brand name, a logo, a symbol, the letters and the slogan contributing to awareness building about the brand and its image. Brand success depends on financial organisation capability to fulfil its promises.

Banking system plays a very important role in economic development. This book will certainly help in understanding the brand management and its utilisation in the banking sector. This main goal of this book is to examine the customer perception and satisfaction towards brand management in commercial banks.

This main goal of this book is to examine the importance of Brand Management in Commercial Banks. The study has covered with the relevant institutions such as banks, customers and Bank brand building practices.

Acknowledgement

First and foremost, I owe it all to my **Satguru** for granting me the wisdom, health and strength to undertake this work task and enabling me to its successful completion of this work.

On a personal note, I am indebted and don't know to express my thanks to My **Mentor** for the overall moral support which made it possible for me to see the light of the day and to my **Parents**, my **Husband** and my **Daughter** for their patience, support and encouragement for publishing this book.

During my earlier academic days in schooling and graduation times, I used to think about doing doctorate and it was a dream for me. But today, my dream has become true because of Research Supervisor **Dr.R. Shunmughan** whose encouragement and guidance have been a source of deep and heartfelt inspiration to me.

I am grateful to the **Principal** for his encouragement, inspiration and for his interest in successfully completing this book.

I would like to express my gratitude to the many people who saw me through this book and all those who provided support, talked things over, read, wrote, offered comments, allowed me to quote their remarks and assisted in the editing, proofreading and design.

Finally, I thank the **Bonfring Publications** for publishing this book in a wonderful manner.

Dr.R. Shophiya

CHAPTER I

INTRODUCTION AND DESIGN OF THE STUDY

1.1. Introduction

The financial sector is a crucial sector of any economy, affecting its business environment, investment, economic prospects and social dimension. Financial sector is important to monitor and compare across economies and over time. There is an indirect impact of financial sector in economic performance of the country. An efficient financial sector reduces the cost and risk of producing and trading goods and services. It makes an important contribution to raising the standard of living of the country by increasing the savings, facilitating foreign capital and financial sector reforms can boost up growth in long run. The key institutional players of financial system are the Central bank, Commercial and Merchant banks, Savings institutions, development financial institutions, insurance companies, mortgage entities, pension funds and financial market institutions.

Indian financial system is strong, diverse, efficient and flexible and is critical to our national objectives of creating a market-driven, productive and competitive economy. Indian financial system supports higher levels of investment and promotes growth in the economy with its depth and coverage. The financial system in India comprises of financial institutions, financial markets, financial instruments and services. The Indian financial system consists of two major segments viz., an organised sector and a traditional sector that is also known as informal credit market. Financial intermediation in the organised sector is conducted by a large number of financial institutions which business organisations are providing financial services to the community. Financial institutions are further classified as banking and non banking entities. The Reserve Bank of India (RBI) as the main regulator of credit is the apex institution in the financial system. Other important financial institutions are the commercial banks (in the public and private sector), cooperative banks, regional rural banks and development banks. Non-bank financial institutions include finance and leasing companies and other institutions like LIC, GIC, UTI, Mutual funds, Provident Funds, Post Office Banks etc.

The banking system is the most dominant segment of the financial sector, accounting for over 80 per cent of the funds flowing through the financial sector. The aggregate deposits of the scheduled commercial banks (SCBs) crose from Rs.5,05,599 crore in March 1997 to Rs.11,03,360 crore in March 2002 representing a rise of 17 per cent. During the same period, the credit portfolio (food and non-food) of SCBs grew from Rs.2,78,401 crore to Rs. 5,89,723 crore, i.e. by 16 per cent. The net profits of SCBs witnessed a noticeable upturn from Rs.6,903 crore in 2013-14 to Rs.18, 572 crore in 2013- 14. The extent and coverage of the banking system can be gauged from the fact that the number of branches of SCBs grew from 8045 in 1969 to 66,186. While rural branches constituted 49 per cent of the total in 2014, semi-urban branches accounted for 28 per cent, urban branches accounted for 19 per cent and metropolitan branches accounted for 16 per cent. As regards the capital market, the resource mobilization from the primary market by non-government public limited companies has declined in the recent past from the high levels witnessed between 1992-93 and 1996-97. Resource mobilization of these companies in the public issues market stood at Rs. 5,692 crore in 2013-14 registering an increase of 19.4 per cent over the amount mobilized during the previous year. The public issues market has been dominated by debt issues both in the private and public sectors in the recent past. In recent years, private placement has emerged as an important vehicle for raising resources by banks, financial institutions and public and private sector companies. Such placements continued to dominate the primary market although the pace of growth of the private placement market has slackened during the last two years. Resource mobilization by mutual funds is an important activity in the capital markets. Although there has been a decline in the net resource mobilization by mutual funds to the extent of 28 per cent during 2013-14, according to SEBI, outstanding net assets of all mutual funds stood at Rs.1,00,594. The strong potential of the capital market as an area of resource mobilization needs no emphasis and this segment of the financial sector would continue to play a significant role in the future[1].

Activities of the commercial banks in India are expanding at a rapid speed after Independence. There is territorial as well as functional expansion of the activities of the bank. Banks which are conservative and conventional in their approach have come out from their shell and face the challenges of planned economic growth. In recent years non-conventional sectors are receiving the attention of commercial banks in India. A better understanding of the implications of financing nonconventional sector by commercial banks is possible only if one looks back the position of commercial banks during the pre-nationalization era. Commercial Banks are is the institutions that ordinarily accept deposits from the people and advances loans. Commercial Banks have been established in accordance with the provisions of the Banking Regulation Act, 1949. Commercial Banks may be Scheduled Banks of Non-Scheduled Banks.

---

[1] www.planningcommission.nic.in

Brand is not only an efficient tool for managers in competitive markets, but also helps the banks in creating more value for customers and creates sustainable competitive advantages. Brand name is essential for factors such as perceived quality, tendency to pay higher prices and product differentiation. Creating a powerful brand over time instead of short-term strategies has been taken into consideration by many banks. It is brand that creates real value in the minds of customers. Therefore, intangible assets are replacing tangible assets. Brand is considered as the most valuable of intangible assets.

The position of brand in business has expanded to such an extent that modern management can be called brand management. Brand can create such issues as customer loyalty, responses to price changes and market outlooks evaluation in the organization. On the other hand, the banking industry is, one of the main foundations of the economy of our country.

In order to accelerates performance speed and to increases customer satisfaction, the identity and status of a brand in the mind of the society and specially the potential and actual customers of banks is mandatory. In this context, it becomes essential to study the perception of the customers towards brand management in commercial banks.

1.2.   Statement of the Problem

Effective banking system is essential for a healthy economy. The banking system of India should not only be hassle free but it should be able to meet new challenges posed by the technology and any other external and internal factors. For the past three decades India's banking system has several outstanding achievements to its credit. The most striking is its extensive reach. It is no longer confined to only metropolitans or cosmopolitans in India. In fact, Indian banking system has reached even to the remote corners of the country. This is one of the reasons of India's growth process.

Indian banking sector can be classified into (1) public sector banks (2) private sector banks (3) foreign banks and (4) co-operative banks. Co-operative banks in India are generally regional/local players. There is no availability of foreign banks in Erode district. Hence this study on service branding of banks focuses on public and private sector banks.

In a highly viable marketing environment, it is very essential that banks differentiate themselves from each other. The product and services of banks can be simply copied. Banking services which are generally intangible require creation of popular image in the minds of consumers which can be done by improving unique brand identity.

In the services literature, banking is classified under "pure service". The quality of the bank brand decides how far the brand factor has contributed successfully to market, so that the bank brand achieves unique, favorable and powerful positioning and customer acceptance. Indian banking industry had taken up well-built branding initiatives in recent years. The brand building activities of private and public sector banks is considered to be the need of the hour. In this regard, the following questions arise:

1) How does brand management in commercial banks ensure progress and development?

2) What is the perception of the customers about brand management in commercial banks?

3) What is the attitude level of the customers towards brand management in commercial banks?

4) How far the customers are satisfied with the brand management of commercial banks?

1.3. Review of Previous Studies

The review of previous studies is considered as important for every research to carry on the study successfully. It helps to know the problem in-depth, the methodology followed and to recognize the unexplored part of the field of study under consideration. In this regard, a review of some of the present study is summarized in this section.

De Chernatony and Dall'Olmo Riley[1]**(1997)** described brand as a multi dimensional construct having nine dimensions which were classified under 3 categories viz., input, output and evolutionary perspectives. The input perspective is company oriented, the output perspective is customer oriented while the evolutionary perspectives is the long term orientation of the brand as an evolving identity. The nine brand dimensions are Legal instrument, Logo, Company, Identity, Image, Personality, Relationship, Added Value, and Evolving entity.

Chernatony and Riley [2]**(1998)** conducted a study titled 'Modeling the components of the brand'. A brand is a multidimensional construct whereby managers augment products or services with values and facilitates the process by which consumers confidently recognize and appreciate these values.

---

[1] De Chernatony and Dall'Olmo Riley, (1997), "The Chasm between Managers' and Consumers Views of Brands: the Experts Perspective", *Journal of Strategic Marketing*, Vol.5, No.2, pp. 89-104.

[2] De Chernatony and Riley, (1998), "Modelling the Components of the Brand", *European Journal of Marketing*, Vol.32, No.11/12, p. 1074.

Fiona Harris and Leslie Chernatony[1]**(2001)** in their study explored the implications of corporate branding for the management of inside brand resources. They have fulfilled that some of the mechanisms used to facilitate greater similarity of brand perceptions within the brand team and statement of a brand's identity to employees.

De Chernatony et al.[2] **(2003)** suggested that in comparison with the goods model for brand building, more work is required in terms of organizational culture and internal branding when building service brands. Successful services-branding models do not stress an external orientation, as evident in good branding, but have a balanced internal and external orientation.

Aron O'cass and Debra grace[3] **(2004)** examined the role of marketer-controlled and marketer-uncontrolled communications on consumption-aroused mind-set and service brand attitudes. Data were gathered from customers of specific service brands and comparisons were made across two different service types (retail stores & banks). The findings indicated that advertising has a significant effect on consumption-aroused feelings and service brand attitudes, whereas word-of-mouth communication affects brand attitudes only in terms of bank brands and publicity has aroused feeling or brand attitude.

Debra grace and Aron O'cass[4]**(2005)** examined the effects of three communication avenues, namely controlled communication (advertising/ promotions), uncontrolled communications (word-of-mounth(WOM)/publicity), and brand name, on consumer service brand evaluation. This study employed a quantitative methodology and data were gathered from consumers intercepted in a shopping mall via a self-completed survey.

Debra grace and Aron O'cass[5] **(2005)** in their study focused on development and testing of a model of service branding. This model is tested in the context of service brands such as retail stores and banks and the results indicate that brand evidence core service, employee service, brand name, service cape, price/value for money, self image congruence and feelings, along with advertizing and promotion, significantly influence consumer satisfaction, attitude and behavioural intentions towards the chosen service brand.

[1] Fiona Harris and Leslie de Chernatony, (2001), "Corporate Branding and Corporate Brand Performance", *European Journal of Marketing*, Vol.35, pp. 441-456.

[2] De Chernatony, Drury and Segal-Horn,(2003), "Building a Service Brand : Stages, People & Orientations", *The Service Industries Journal*, pp. 1-21.

[3] Aron O'cass and Debra Grace, (2004), "Service Brands and Communication Effects", *Journal of Marketing Communications*, Vol.10, pp. 241-254.

[4] Debra Grace and Aron O'cass,(2005), "Examining the Effects of Service Brand Communications on Brand Evaluation", *Journal of Product & Brand Management*,Vol.14, pp.106-116.

[5] Debra Grace and O'cass, (2005), "Service Branding: Consumer Verdicts on Service Brands", *Journal of Retailing and Consumer Services*, Vol.12, pp. 125-139.

Grace & O'Cass[1] **(2005)** conducted an empirical investigation of service brands to test their Service Brand Verdict model. The model was tested in the context of service brands such as retail stores and banks. Seven interviews with service brand customers of banks or retail stores were conducted prior to the study to verify whether the 61 dimensions proposed in the framework are relevant to customers. Five national bank brands and Five retail services were chosen for the study. Purposeful sampling technique was used and customers who had used the retail settings or banking services at least one of the brands were chosen to provide the data. The sample sizes for banking survey were 251 and retail services were 269. The results indicated that core service, employee service, brand name, service cape, price/value for money, self-image congruence and feelings, along with advertizing, promotion, brand attitude, customer satisfaction and brand verdict significantly influence and behavioral intentions towards the chosen service brand.

Aurand et al.[2] **(2005)** studied human resource management's role in internal branding. "A two-way e-mail survey was administered to business seminar participants. Systematic random sample of 1177 participants were drawn from a list of business seminar participants of which 922 responded. Multi-item measures and a six point Likert scale were developed and analyzed to better understand the perceived involvement of human resource (HR) in internal branding efforts and the relationship between HR involvement and the incorporation of the brand message into work activities and attitude toward the brand. It was found that in spite of well-documented internal branding initiatives, most of the HR departments were not successful in delivering the corporate branding message. Employees seemed to have a more positive attitude toward the brand and are more likely to incorporate this image into 69 their work activities when there is some degree of HR involvement in the internal branding process".

Vallaster and Chernatony[3]**(2005)** have implied that employees of a service brand are ultimately responsible for delivering the brand promise of the service brand and they are the critically important constituent of the service brand.

Ram Herstein and Eyal Gamliel [4]**(2006)** made a study titled "The role of private branding in improving service quality" to examine the potential contribution of private branding to the service sector, and to integrate private branding into the SERVQUAL model. A total of 300

[1] Grace & O'Cass, (2005), "Service Branding Consumer Verdicts on Service Brands", *Journal of Retailing & Consumer Services,* Vol.12, pp. 125-139.

[2] Aurand T. W., Gorchels L. and Bishop T. R., (2005), "Human Resource Management Role in Internal Branding: An Opportunity for Cross-Functional Brand Message Synergy", *The Journal of Product and Brand Management,* Vol.14, pp. 163–169.

[3] Vallaster and de Chernatony, (2005),"Internal Brand Building and Structuration : the Role of Leadership", *European Journal of Marketing,*Vol.40, No 7/8, pp. 761-784.

[4] Ram Herstein and Eyal Gamliel,(2006), "The Role of Private Branding in Improving Service Quality", *Managing Service Quality: An International Journal,* Vol.16, No.3, pp. 306.

customers of a health maintenance organization (HMO) were asked about the five dimensions of the service-quality model and about several aspects of their HMO's private brand. The study finds that satisfaction with service quality among subjects who were aware of the HMO's private brand was higher than that of unaware subjects when asked directly. In addition, a positive relationship was found between the perceptions of service quality in the HMO and the evaluation of a private brand in the HMO those customers who were aware of the private brand. They concluded that private branding constitutes an additional (sixth) dimension in the SERVQUAL model.

Mosley [1]**(2007)** suggested that employees play a key role in developing sustainable service brand differentiation, through the development of a consistently positive service attitude, and also through the emotional values that tend to be evoked by a particularly distinctive style of service. It is generally agreed that these intangible brand characteristics are far more difficult for competitors to copy than the operational components of a service brand experience.

Loughlin Deirdre and Isabelle Szmigin [2]**(2007)** explored both consumer and employees' views on the role and importance of branding in retail banking. Seven interviews were conducted with employees from the financial services sector. Purposive sampling was done to select the interviews. Questions were posed to financial services managers which included the role and importance of branding within their organization and the impact of their various branding activities on customers. Purposive stratified sampling method was used where 50 consumers, representing the desired range of demographic characteristics (gender, age, profession and product-related criteria participated in the survey). Financial services employees identified a number of issues in the context of branding and brand management. Lack of a coherent brand image for financial services was pointed out by employees. Findings from the customer survey indicated that branding was used selectively by customers for evaluation of the financial services. Customers rated functional services to be far more important than emotional connect.

Ceridwyn King and Debra Grace[3]**(2008)** conducted a study titled "Internal branding : Exploring the employee's perspective". The creation of a strong brand and the deliverance of perceived service quality are premised by employees' ability to deliver on customer expectations. They explored the differential effect that internally oriented initiatives have on

---

[1] Mosley,(2007), " Customer Experience, Organization Culture & the Employer Brand", *The Journal of Product and Brand Management,* Vol.15, No.2, pp. 123-134.

[2] O'loughlin Deirdre and Isabelle Szmigin, (2007), "Services Branding: Revealing The Rhetoric Within Retail Banking", *The Service Industries Journal,* Vol.27, No.4, pp. 435–452.

[3] Ceridwyn king and Debra grace,(2008), "Internal Branding: Exploring the Employee's Perspective", *Journal of Brand Management,* Vol.15, pp. 358-372.

an organization's human capital and its subsequent impact on the organization's brand, from the employee's perspective.

Noel Albert et al. [1](2008) in their study mentioned that consumers may develop feelings of love toward some brands, but the meaning and underlying dimensions of this construct require further development. Through an exploratory Internet study of 843 respondents in France, this research used both qualitative and quantitative approaches to explore the concept of love. Eleven dimensions emerge through a correspondence analysis and the concomitant use of a multiple correspondence analysis and cluster analysis of the wording that respondents use to describe their feeling of love and the special type of relationships they have with the brands they love. These dimensions identified in France compared dimensions of love found in previous research conducted in the United States.

Mohammad Reza Jalilvand et al. [2](2008) in their study aimed to integrate consumer-based brand equity for a tourism destination (CBBETD) and the theory of planned behavior (TPB) to examine the relationship between branding and customers' attitudes toward banking services. Data were collected from 364 customers and analyzed by hierarchical regression approach. Branding constructs including brand image, brand awareness, perceived quality and brand loyalty have a significant relationship with attitude constructs including affective attitude, subjective norm, perceived behavioral control and behavioral intention.

Margit Raich and Marc-Philipp Crepaz [3](2009) conducted a study titled "Fitting new brand principles: First encounter at bank branches". Market developments in the financial industries have forced banks to rethink their strategic positioning. One possibility for achieving uniqueness in the retail banking market is to develop an explicit brand strategy. If service quality and customer relationships, which have been identified as essential elements for the enduring success of retail banks, are the key characteristics of brand strategy, a customer-oriented culture is needed to transfer the brand principles. If the experiences concerning the services are insufficiently rewarding, the customers can be expected to break their relationships with the bank. To guarantee an optimal service quality, it will be helpful to measure the services offered by identifying the strengths and the weaknesses in the

---

[1] Noel Albert, Dwight Merunka and Pierre Valette-Florence, (2008), "When Consumers Love their Brands: Exploring the Concept and its Dimensions", *Journal of Business Research*, Vol.61, pp. 1062-1075.

[2] Mohammad Reza Jalilvand, Arash Shahin and Leila Nasrolahi Vosta ,(2008), " Examining the Relationship between Branding and Customers' Attitudes toward Banking Services: Empirical Evidence from Iran", *International Journal of Islamic and Middle Eastern Finance and Management*, Vol.7, pp. 214 – 227.

[3] Margit Raich and Marc-Philipp. Crepaz, (2009), " Fitting New Brand Principles: First Encounter at Bank Branches", *Journal of Brand Management*, Vol.16, pp. 480-491.

performances concerning the brand strategy. For this reason, mystery shopping can be used to analyze the perceived quality of the delivery of services.

Natalie Mizik and Robert Jacobson[1] **(2009)** attempted to develop and validate a conditional multiplier approach for valuing branded business. The approach enhances traditional multiplier- based valuation by explicit incorporating brand characteristics into the model. The study finds that brand metrics have statistically significant associations with valuation multipliers and incremental explanatory power to accounting variables in explaining valuation multiplier.

Lars Ohnemus[2]**(2009)** in his study titled "Is branding creating shareholder wealth for banks?" analyzed, shareholder perspective, the link between branding and financial performance. He pointed out that, in the European context, on situations in which shareholder wealth is created or destroyed, and this is measured by using return on assets or market-to-book value as a performance benchmark. The investigation is designed as a quantitative study and is based on responses obtained from 847 listed banks including 480 located in Europe. There is an analysis of the correlation between branding and shareholder value, by means of regression analysis. Deductions are made for key variables including capital structure, ownership and capital market ratios.

Christodoulides George and De Chernatony Leslie[3] **(2010)** conducted a study on "Consumer-based brand equity conceptualization and measurement". They brought together the scattered literature on consumer based brand equity's conceptualization and measurement. Measures of consumer based brand equity are classified as either direct or indirect. Indirect measures assess consumer-based brand equity through its demonstrable dimensions and are superior from a diagnostic level.

Jennifer et al.[4]**(2010)** indicated that linguistic characteristics of brand names can cognitively affect product evaluations. The results reveal across multiple brand names and product categories that exposure to a brand name that has sound repetition in its phonetic structure and is spoken aloud produces positive affect, which favorably affects consumers' brand evaluations, reactions to cross-selling, and product choice. The effects are moderated by

---

[1] Natalie Mizik and Robert Jacobson,(2009), "Valuing Branded Businesses", *Journal of Marketing*, Vol.73, No.6,pp. 137-153.

[2] Lars Ohnemus,(2009), "Is branding Creating Shareholder Wealth for Banks?", *International Journal of Bank Marketing*, Vol.27, No.3, p. 186.

[3]Christodoulides George and De Chernatony Leslie,(2010),"Consumer-Based Brand Equity Conceptualization and Measurement", *International Journal of Research in Marketing*, Vol.1, No.52, pp. 43-66.

[4] Jennifer J.Argo, Monica Popa and Malcolm C.Smith, (2010),"The Sound of Brands", *Journal of Marketing*, Vol.74, No.4, pp. 97-109.

consumer 'sensitivity to repetition, consumer 'opportunity to experience emotions, and the degree to which the brand name's phonetic sound repetition deviates from linguistic expectations.

Habibollah Javanmard and Ensiyeh Nemati Nia[1] **(2011)** in their article aimed to investigate the effect of internal branding on employees' perception, brand commitment, brand loyalty and performance of banks in attracting customers, in Islamic banking. The randomly selected samples include employees of Islamic banks located in Iran. A total of 350 questionnaires were distributed to employees of Islamic banks. The study revealed that the organization brand is effective on brand identification from the employees' perspective and on their brand commitment, but it has no meaningful effect on loyalty and performance of employees.

Robert Hinson et al.[2]**(2011)** in their paper titled "Brands and service quality perception" attempted to determine from the standpoint of undergraduate students, service quality dispositions of bank brands operating in Ghana. A structured questionnaire containing 12 service quality statements was designed and administered to 519 first time undergraduate bank customers to measure their perception of service quality regard to bank brands in ghana. They concluded that service knowledge dimension of brand service quality as the weakest performance service attribute for banks operating in Ghana.

Rajeev Batra et al.[3]**(2012)** conducted a study on "Brand Love" and investigated the nature and consequences of brand love. Arguing that research on brand love needs to be built on an understanding of how consumers actually experience this phenomenon, they conduct two qualitative studies to uncover the different elements of the consumer prototype of brand love. Then, they use structural equations modeling on survey data to explore how these elements can be modeled as both first-order and integration, passion-driven behaviors, positive emotional connection, long-term relationship, positive overall attitude valence, attitude certainty and confidence, and anticipated separation distress. In addition to these seven core elements of brand love itself, the prototype includes quality beliefs as an antecedent of brand love and brand loyalty, word of mouth, and resistance to negative information as outcomes. Both the first order and higher-order brand love models predict loyalty, word of mouth, and

---

[1] Habibollah Javanmard and Ensiyeh Nemati Nia,(2011), "Effects on Internal Branding on Brand Supporting Behaviours of Employees Regarding Customer Attraction in Islamic Banks", *The IUP Journal of Brand Management*,Vol.8, p. 35.

[2] Robert Hinson, N.Owusu Frimpong and Julius Dasah, (2011),"Brands and Service Quality Perception", *Marketing Intelligence & Planning,* Vol.29, No.3, p. 264.

[3] Rajeev Batra, Aaron Ahuvia and Richard P.Bagozzi,(2010), "Brand Love", *Journal of Marketing*, Vol.76, No.1, pp. 1-16.

resistance better, and provide a greater understanding, than an overall summary measure of brand love.

Ceridwyn King et al.[1]**(2014)** conducted a study entitled "Employee brand equity: Scale development and validation". The study focused on the internal brand management (IBM) literature through the conceptualization and operationalisation of the 'employee brand equity' construct in order to assess the effectiveness of IBM activities. The aim of the study is to develop and validate an employee brand equity (EBE) scale. It includes a four-phase proces, with four data collections using a total of 752 respondents. The data analyses indicate that the resulting 11-items (3-factor) EBE scale has face, content, convergent and discriminate validity and is reliable across the samples.

Olokoyo Omowunmi Felicia et al.[2] **(2012)** examined the impacts of the global financial crisis on the Nigerian banking industry with particular emphasis on branding of bank services. The objective of the study is to determine what effects the crisis had on the Nigerian economy and to examine its effects on branding of bank services. It also focused on measures put in place to mitigate the negative effects of economic meltdown by the central bank of Nigeria. Primary data were generated through in-depth interview and the use of the questionnaire. The study employed the use of chi-square in analyzing the data obtained. The findings of this study pointed out the fact that the global economic meltdown had a deteriorating effect on all sectors in the economy and had a greater effect on the financial sector in Nigeria most especially the banking sector. However, this economic meltdown has a positive effect on branding of bank services. Banks are investing on branding more than ever before, in order to survive the turbulent environment. It is therefore recommended that the regulators of the banking sector need to strengthen their legal framework in order to close all avenues which may create gaps for unethical practices to take place. Managements of banks are also encouraged to embrace internal marketing in order to promote excellent service culture.

Joana Cesar Machado et al.[3]**(2012)** explored how name and logo design characteristics, and specifically figurativeness, influence consumer preferences in the context of a brand merger, in the banking sector. The results suggested that there is a clear preference for figurative logo. Furthermore, there is evidence that logos may be as important as the company

---

[1] Ceridwyn King, Debra Grace and Daniel C Funk, (2012), "Employee Brand Equity: Scale Development and Validation", *Journal of Brand Management*, Vol.19, pp. 268-288.

[2] Olokoyo Omowunmi Felicia, Ogunnaike and Olaleke Oluseye,(2012), "Global Economi Meltdown and its Perceived Effects on Branding of Bank Services in Nigeria", Directory of Open Access Journal, Vol.5,No.1,p. 30.

[3] Joana Cesar Machado, Leonor Vacas-de-Carvalho, Patrício Costa and Paulo Lencastre,(2012), "Brand Mergers: Examining Consumers' Responses to Name and Logo Design", *Journal of Product and Brand Management*, Vol. 21, No.6, p. 418.

name in a merger situation, in terms of assuring consumers that there remains a connection to the brand's past. They concluded that the logo chosen by consumers reflects their aesthetic responses, whereas the selected name reflects their evaluation of the brand's offers or its presence in the market.

Rinalini Kakati and Smritishikh Choudhury (2013)[1] in their research paper evaluated global and Indian brands in the Consumer Durables Sector by using Customer-Based Brand Equity Model. Six brand building blocks, Brand Salience, Brand Imagery, Brand Performance, Brand Judgment, Brand Feelings and Brand Resonance. The findings reveal that global brand's brand strength is much higher than the Indian brand's. The Indian brand has scored significantly less in 'Brand Preference' and consequently its 'Brand Strength' has been much lesser than that of the global brand. Two other hypotheses were also tested regarding the existence of positive relationship between brand trust and brand affect and attitudinal loyalty and purchase loyalty. The need to test these hypotheses arise because of the importance of the last brand building block, 'Brand Resonance', to marketing managers, as high brand resonance implies high loyalty. The study concluded that there exists a positive relationship between brand trust and brand affect and attitudinal and purchase loyalty for both global and Indian brand.

Zahra Poorkarimi Kokand and Zeinolabedin Amini sabegh[2]**(2013)** in their study investigated the effect of relationship marketing on brand loyalty of bank customers. 384 questionnaires consisting of 20 questions in order to test the hypotheses were distributed among customers of Bank Refah Kargaran in four areas of Tehran. The method was descriptive survey method and sampling method was a multi- stage random sampling. Pearson correlation test and regression and SPSS 16 software were used in order to test hypotheses and analyze the collected data. They concluded that variables of Trust - Commitment – Communication, which are the foundations of relationship marketing, have a significant impact on customer satisfaction and brand loyalty. Another finding of the study is that the variable of customer loyalty is an important factor in customer satisfaction.

Johnson Yeboah et al.[3]**(2014)** explored the differential effect that internally oriented initiatives have on an organization's human capital and its subsequent impact on the organization's brand. A case study approach is adopted using a qualitative methodology. In-

---

[1] Rinalini P Kakati and Smritishikh Choudhury,(2013), "Measuring Customer-Based Brand Equity Through Brand Building Blocks for Durables", *The IUP Journal of brand management,* Vol.10, No.2, p. 5.

[2] Zahra Poorkarimi kokand, and Zeinolabedin amini sabegh,(2013), "Effect of Relationship Marketing on Brand Loyalty between Customers of Bank Refah Kargaran in Tehran city – Iran", *IOSR Journal of Business and Management,* 62-66.

[3] Johnson Yeboah, George Dominic Ewur, Evelyn Delali Adigbo and Ernest K. Asirifi,(2014), "Internal Branding in a Service Industry- A Case of Banks in Ghana", *European Scientific Journal,* Vol.10, No.7, pp. 218-238.

depth interviews reveal that employees feel that their actions are vital to the brand, and findings from a survey of 500 respondents demonstrate positive relationships among internal branding and their brand promise delivery. The study also helps to emphasize the importance of internal branding for customer attraction in the banking industry.

De Chernatony et al.[1]**(2003)** suggested that in comparison with the goods model for brand building, more work is required in terms of organizational culture and internal branding when building service brands. Successful services-branding models do not stress an external orientation, as evident in good branding, but have a balanced internal and external orientation.

Opoku et al.[2]**(2008)** studied the impact of internal marketing on the perception of service quality in retail banking services in Ghana. The study took a case study approach in which Ghana Commercial Bank Limited was studied. Stratified sampling was followed to collect data. A survey of 32 top managers, 100 employees and 200 external customers of the bank was undertaken to assess the impact of internal marketing on the perception of service quality. The internal customers' (employees) instrument consisted of dimensions such as internal marketing, service quality and, demographic details. The external customer instrument consisted of two sections which were service quality and demographics. The results suggested that internal marketing influenced service quality.

Anber Abraheem Shlash Mohammad and Shireen Yaseen Mohammad Alhamadani[3] **(2011)** analyzed five dimension of service quality viz., Reliability, Responsiveness, Empathy, Assurance, and Tangibles. Customer satisfaction was measured by a nine items adopted. 260 questionnaires were distributed randomly to customers of commercial banks branches located (thirteen commercial banks in Jordan) in IRBID (A city of Jordan). Multiple regression analysis was employed to test the impact of service quality on customer satisfaction. They suggested that service quality is an important antecedent of customer satisfaction.

---

[1] De Chernatony, Drury and Segal-Horn,(2003), "Building a Service Brand : Stages, People & Orientations", *The Service Industries Journal*, pp. 1-21.

[2] Opoku, Robert Ankomah, Nana Atuobi-Yiadom, Cathryn Serwaah Chong and Russell Abratt, (2008), "The Impact of Internal Marketing on the Perception of Service Quality in Retail Banking: A Ghanaian Case", *Journal of Financial Services Marketing*, Vol.13, pp. 317–329.

[3] Anber Abraheem Shlash Mohammad and Shireen Yaseen Mohammad Alhamadani, (2011), "Service Quality Perspectives and Customer Satisfaction in Commercial Banks Working in Jordan", *Middle Eastern Finance and Economics*,

Abdelghani Echchabi and Hassanuddeen Abd Aziz[1]**(2012)** examined the willingness of the Moroccan customers to adopt Islamic banking services and the factors that may influence their decision. A total of 200 questionnaires were randomly distributed to Moroccan banking customers, out of which 146 were properly filled and returned. Multiple regression and one sample t-test were subsequently applied. The result that uncertainty, relative advantage, compatibility, awareness as well as subjective norm, have a significant impact on the attitude towards Islamic banking services in Morocco. Likewise, normative belief was also found to have a significant influence on subjective norm, with particular reference to the parents, siblings, peers and colleagues, as the main referent groups. In addition, facilitating conditions was found to have a significant influence on perceived behavioural control and finally attitude, subjective norm and perceived behavioural control were found to have a significant impact on the intention to adopt Islamic banking services in Morocco. It is worth noting that complexity does not have any influence on attitude and self efficacy does not have any influence on perceived behavioural control as well. On the other hand, the results show that the Moroccan customers are willing to shift to Islamic banking services, with a slight preference of long run adoption i.e. three years and above. This study is one of the earliest to be conducted on customers' perception and willingness to adopt Islamic banking services in Morocco.

Sunday Samson Babalola [2]**(2009)** examined the influence of perceived financial distress and customers' attitude towards banking in Nigeria. 201 bank customers made up of 144 males and 57 females drawn from 27 banks in Logos participated in the study. He suggested that perceived financial distress and bank account customer had significant main effect on attitude toward banking.

Arun kumar et al.[3]**(2010)** in their study endeavored to fill the gap in the service quality which determines customer satisfaction and attitudinal loyalty literature by exploring the dimensions of customer perceived service quality in the context of Indian retail banking industry. A set of variables were drawn from customer's perceptions about service quality. These parameters had been used in the context of two of largest private banks dealing with retailing banking namely, ICICI & HDFC to identity the underlying dimensions of service quality which determine customer satisfaction and attitudinal loyalty. The study emphasized

---

[1] Abdelghani Echchabi and Hassanuddeen Abd Aziz,(2012), "Empirical Investigation of Customers' Perception and Adoption Towards Islamic Banking Services in Morocco", *Middle-East Journal of Scientific Research*, Vol.12, pp. 849-858.

[2] Sunday Samson Babalola,(2009),"Perception of Financial Distress and Customers' Attitude Towards Banking", *International Journal of Business and Management*, Vol.4, No.10, p 6.

[3] Arun kumar .S, Tamilmani .B, Mahalingam .S and Vanjikovan .M ,(2010), "Influence of Service Quality on Attitudinal Loyalty in Private Retail Banking: An Empirical Study" ,*The Journal of Management Research*, Vol.9, No.4, pp. 21-38.

that to gain and sustain the competitive advantages in the fast changing retail banking industry in india, it was found crucial for private banks to understand what customers perceive to be the key dimensions of service quality and what impact the identified dimensions might have on customer's attitudinal loyalty. The study found out that the customers distinguish 5 dimensions of service quality in the case of private retail banking. Furthermore, the results yielded an intricate pattern of service quality-attitudinal loyalty relationship at the level of the overall dimensions. They suggested that these issues should be of a central concern for retail bank, managers as well as service management academics and practitioners to explore the specific component and should train their employees in those areas to delight the customers in the needed domain to enhance service quality and build attitudinal loyalty to retain the valued customers, the most profitable customers, for the banks.

Mohammad Reza Jalilvand et al.[1]**(2011)** mentioned that branding is to differentiate a product or service from others and creating a unique brand image of a certain product or service in the minds of target market. Their research integrates consumer-based brand equity and the theory of planned behavior in evaluating the performance of Iran's Melli bank in branding and measures the impact of branding on customers' attitudes. A field survey was conducted on Iran's Melli bank in Isfahan, the biggest national bank in Iran. Data were collected and analyzed from 314 prospective customers. Findings indicate that Iran's Melli bank has performed unsatisfactorily in presenting a desired image to the target market. They concluded that Melli bank needs to strengthen its brand loyalty by improving its quality of banking services and marketing communications.

Johnson[2]**(1995)** found that the determinants of service quality revealed that there are some service quality determinants of internet banking, namely satisfier and dis- satisfiers. The main sources of satisfaction are attentiveness, responsiveness, care and friendliness. The main sources of dissatisfaction are integrity, reliability, responsiveness, availability & functionality.

Parimal vyas[3]**(2000)**conducted a study on "measurement of customer satisfaction: A study on banking services". The study attempted to study empirically, customers satisfaction from the services provided by different banks and also to analyze the response of customers towards the actual time taken by banks and co-operative banks need to improve on reducing

[1] Mohammad Reza Jalilvand ,Farhad Ebrahimabadi and Neda Samiei,(2011), "The Impact of Branding on Customers' Attitudes toward Banking Services" (The Case of Iran's Melli Bank), *International Business and Management,* Vol. 2, No.1, pp. 186-197.

[2] Johnson R,(1995), "The determinants of Service Quality: Satisfier & Dissatisfier", *International Journal of Service Industry Management,*Vol.6, No.5, pp. 53-71.

[3] Parimal Vyas, (2000), "Measurement of Customer Satisfaction: A Study on Banking Services", *Business Perspectives,* Vol.4, pp. 73-87.

the overall time taken to complete banking transaction comparatively the private and foreign banks had taken much lesse time for completing their transaction. She suggested that the nationalized commercial banks and co-operative banks had to increase the use of information, technology and CRM to deliver standardized services to its target customers.

Shajahan[1](2005) analyzed customer satisfaction on various modes of banking services. He concluded the study with 100 account holders of ICICI bank in Chennai. The study revealed that internet internet banking increased the level of satisfaction among the bank customers. He was of the opinion that the internet literacy was the major factor underlying online banking in penetration in India.

Mishra and Jain[2](2007) studied various dimensions of customer satisfaction in nationalized and private sector banks. The study concluded that satisfaction of the customers is an invaluable asset for the modern organizations, providing unmatched competitive edge, which help in building long term relationship as well as brand equity.

Manoj Kumar Joshi[3](2008) in his article entitled as "Customer Service in Retail Banking in India" deals with the service aspects of banks in retail banking. It attempts to highlight that customer service of high standard and quality implemented through the use of modern technology helps banks to succeed in the competitive world of retail banking. Banks should also provide comprehensive information to the borrowers with regard to the fees / charges levied while processing the loans. Banks, by standardizing the procedures, shall make the customer's visit to banks hassle free and direct them to the right officials to save the customers from making time-consuming enquiries.

Sultan Singh[4](2009) in his paper entitled, "Impact of ATM on Customer Satisfaction" highlights the impact of ATM on customer satisfaction. It is a comparative study of three major banks i.e. SBI, ICICI Bank and HDFC Bank. It includes the review of the various services provider by the three banks. A sample of 360 respondents equally representing each bank has been taken through questionnaire which shows the level of satisfaction among different customers.

---

[1] Shajahan.S,(2005), "A Study on the Level of Customer Satisfaction on Various Modes of Banking Services in India", *The ICFAI journal of bank management*, Vol.4, p.79.

[2] Mishra J.K. and Jain M , (2007), "Constituent Dimensions of Customer Satisfaction: A Study of Nationalized & Private Banks", *Prajnan*, Vol.35, pp. 390-398.

[3] Manoj Kumar Joshi, (2008),"Customer Services in Retail Banking in India", *ICFAI University Press*, Hyderabad, pp. 59-68.

[4] Sultan Singh and Komal,(2009), "Impact of ATM on Customer Satisfaction", *Business Intelligence Journal*, Vol.2, No.2, pp. 276-287.

Sandip Ghosh and Kailash Srivastava [1]**(2010)** in their study "Impact of Service Quality on Customer Satisfaction, Loyalty, and Commitment in the Indian Banking Sector", examined the strength of association among the independent variable, namely service quality perception and dependent variables namely customer satisfaction, customer loyalty and customer commitment. They concluded that customer value four dimensions of perceived service quality: assurance, empathy, tangibles, security and reliability. The result also showed significant differences between public and private sector banks with regard to customer satisfaction, commitment and two dimensions of loyalty namely, loyalty to company and willingness to pay. Public sector banks should focus on assurance – empathy, tangibles and the private sector banks should focus on providing reliable services.

Waqarul ul Haq and Bakhtiar Muhammad[2]**(2012)** in their study compared public and private sector banks of Pakistan by evaluating their customer satisfaction. This research has mainly based on primary data collected through a well-structured questionnaire (adopted from three different studies). The questionnaire was distributed to 351 different respondents on different chosen locations. The study made a useful contribution as there are only a few number of studies conducted in Pakistan on the areas like price, technology, reliability, customer service, location and infrastructure. The authors suggested that customer satisfaction varies from person to person and, bank managers need to conduct more researches in order to evaluate customer satisfaction more strongly.

Mesay Sata Shanka[3]**(2012)** conducted a study entitled "Bank Service Quality, Customer Satisfaction and Loyalty in Ethiopian Banking Sector". The major aim of the research paper is to measure the quality of service offered by private banks operating in Ethiopia. Moreover, it tries to investigate the relationship between service quality, customer satisfaction and loyalty. The five dimensions of SERVPERF model i.e. reliability, assurance, tangibility, empathy and responsiveness were used to measure the quality of service offered by the private banks. In order to achieve the aims, both primary and secondary sources of data were used. The primary data were collected through administrating questionnaire. Convenient sampling procedure was used to obtain 260 responses from customer of banking services in Hawassa city on the 22 items, SERVPERF scale measure perception regarding their respective banks service.

---

[1] Sandip Ghosh Hazra and Dr. Kailash B.L. Srivastava,(2010), "Impact of Service Quality on Customer Satisfaction, Loyality and Commitment in the Indian Banking Sector", *Indian Journal of Marketing*, West Bengal.

[2] Waqar ul Haq and Bakhtiar Muhammad, (2012), "Customer Satisfaction: A Comparison of Public and Private Banks Of Pakistan", *IOSR Journal of Business and Management,*Vol.1, pp. 1-5.

[3] Mesay sata shanka, (2012), "Bank Service Quality, Customer Satisfaction and Loyalty in Ethiopian Banking Sector", *Journal of Business Administration and Management Science Research*, Vol. 1(1), pp. 001-009.

Correlation and multiple regressions were used to investigate the relationship between dependent and independent variables. The correlation results indicate that there is a positive correlation between the dimensions of service quality and customer satisfaction. He suggested that offering quality service have positive impact on overall customer satisfaction. The research proves that empathy and responsiveness plays the most important role in customer satisfaction level followed by tangibility, assurance, and finally the bank reliability. The research findings also indicate offering high quality service increase customer satisfaction, which in turn leads to high level of customer commitment and loyalty.

Doddaraju [1]**(2013)** in his study titled 'Customer satisfaction towards public and private sector banking services with special reference to the Anantpur District of Andhra Pradesh' concluded that satisfaction level with regard to public sector units courtesy shown by bank staff at the counter is very low. Therefore, the banks should pay special attention to "Human Resource Development" by giving timely training to the employees to conduct themselves better.

Ahmad Jamal and Kamal Naser [2]**(2013)** in their study focused on Customer's satisfaction in retail banking. A total of 300 questionnaires were randomly distributed to customers of a specific bank in Pakistan. Results indicate that there was a strong relationship between service quality and customer satisfaction. There was, however, no relationship between customer satisfaction and tangible aspects of the service environment.

Cronin and Taylor [3]**(1992)** in their study investigate the conceptualization and measurement of service quality and the relationships between service quality, consumer satisfaction, and purchase intentions. They suggested that the current operationalization of service quality confounds satisfaction and attitude. Hence, the authors test (1) an alternative method of operationalizing perceived service quality and (2) the significance of the relationships between service quality, consumer satisfaction, and purchase intentions. The results suggest that (1) a performance-based measure of service quality may be an improved means of measuring the service quality construct, (2) service quality is an antecedent of consumer satisfaction,(3) consumer satisfaction has a significant effect on purchase intentions, and (4) service quality has less effect on purchase intentions than consumer satisfaction.

---

[1]M. E. Doddaraju,(2013), "A study on Customer Satisfaction towards Public and Private Sector Banking Services", *Global Journal of Management and Business Studies,* Vol.3,No.3, pp. 287-294.

[2] Ahmad Jamal and Kamal Nasar,(2013), "Factors Influencing Customer Satisfaction in the Retail Banking Sector in Pakistan", *International Journal of Commerce and Management,* Vol.13, No.2, p. 29.

[3] Cronin J. J. and Taylor, S. A.,(1992), "Measuring Service Quality: A Maximisation and Extension", *Journal of Marketing,* Vol. 56, No.3, pp. 55-68.

Debra grace and Aron O'cass[1] (2004) conducted a study entitled "Examining service experiences and post – consumption evaluations". The impact of the service experience on consumers' feelings, satisfaction and service brand attitudes are of vital importance to service marketers. This study seeks to explore the dimensions of the service brand that influence consumers at time of service consumption. The study also examines post-consumption evaluations. A study of 254 bank consumers revealed that the core service, employee service and services cape make a significant contribution to the service consumption experience.

Zillur Rahman[2] (2005) in their study measured the services quality of banks in india. He investigated the difference between customers' expectations and perceptions towards the quality of services. The study was conducted using the SERVQUAL instrument. The result indicated that the sample population had perceptual problems with their banking service experiences.

Bhayani[3](2005) in his study entitled, "Empirical Study on Retail Banking Awareness" has focused on the Retail Banking Awareness by conducting a survey on 200 customers having their current accounts with private banks, nationalized and cooperative banks in Rajkot city of Gujarat. The main objectives of his study were to compare the services provided by different private sector banks in the Rajkot City and also to know the customers awareness about the services provided and how often they utilized these services. The study concludes that in India, due to various factors like illiteracy etc, the IT awareness of the customers was still very low. That is why the banks needed to put major efforts towards educating the customers for building up an IT savvy customer base".

Chopra[4] (2006) highlighted the importance of technology in banking services and opined that technology would pave way for business process re-engineering. He observed that public sector banks and old private sector banks were slow to changes in technology in Indian banking sector.

---

[1] Debra grace and Aron O'cass, (2004), PExamining Service Experiences and post - Consumption Evaluations", *Journal of Service Marketing*,Vol.18, pp. 450-461.

[2] Zillur Ram,(2005), "Service Quality: Gaps in the Indian Banking Industries", *ICFAI Journal of Marketing Management* ,Vol.4, pp. 37-47.

[3] Bhayani S.J.,(2005), "Retail Banking Awareness: An Empirical Analysis", *Indian Journal of Marketing,* Vol.31, No.5.

[4] Chopra, (2006), "IT & Business Process Re-Engineering, *Indian Banker.*

Ndubisi[1] **(2006)** studied the antecedents of relationship quality in Malaysian banking sector. Descriptive research design using survey method was followed in this study. Based on the data collected from 220 customers of 15 retail banks in Malaysia, the study found that overall customer satisfaction is a key determinant of relationship quality. 400 customers were approached of which 220 participated in the survey. The indicators of customer satisfaction included trust, commitment, communication, service quality, service satisfaction and conflict handling. These indicators were found to contribute to the overall level of satisfaction of bank customers which in turn was found to determine the perceived quality of the relationship between customers and the bank.

David Sam Jayakumar and Narsis[2] **(2011)** studied the physical and core service quality of State Bank of India (SBI). They undertook a survey by contacting 627 Bank Customers in urban, semi- urban and rural location of the SBI. Stratified random sampling was used. The results found that the service quality of SBI had a positive impact on the satisfaction and commitment of customers.

Asok Sharma et al.[3]**(2012)** revealed the role of CRM in enhancing organizational growth in reference to the banking industry (HDFC) by trend method. The study analysed the actual impact of CRM in enhancing the organizational performance. Some key parameters affecting the organizational growth of the HDFC bank are identified and studied in relation to CRM. Based on the analysis of these relations of the key parameters of growth will be established. Finally the study suggested to adopt specific measures to enhance the impact of CRM in organizational growth of banks.

Sakkthivel[4] **(2006)** studied the impact of demographics in influencing Indian internet users in availing different services online. The study revealed that age and occupation have significant impact on availing different categories of services online which include the banking services. The study also showed the significance of demographics on online consumption of services in the growing Indian market.

---

[1] Ndubisi, (2006), "A Structural Equation Modeling of the Antecedents of Relationship Quality in the Malaysian Banking Sector", *Journal of Financial Services* Marketing, Vol.11,No.2, pp. 131-141.

[2] G.S. David Sam Jayakumar and I. Narsis,(2011), "Physical and Core Services Quality : State Bank of India", *SCMS Journal of Indian Management*, Vol.VIII ,No.IV, p.90.

[3] Dr. Asok Sharma, Dr. Tapasya Julka and Ms.Sonali Bhardwaj,(2012), "Customer Relationship Management: A Growth Catalyst for HDFC Bank", International Journal of Business Economics & Management Research, Vol.2, pp. 149-166.

[4] Sakkthivel,(2006), "Impact of Demographics on the Consumption of Different Online Services in India", *Journal of Internet Banking & Commerce*,Vol.11, No.3, p. 7.

Solomon[1]**(2007)** conducted a study on private and public sector bank managers. An empirical investigation to job characteristics and organizational climate a showed that the private sector professionals were more satisfied than their counterparts in the public sector.

Hugar and Vaz [2]**(2008)** studied the customer orientation in public sector, private sector and foreign banks in India and found that business per employee and profits per employee were found to be highest in foreign banks followed by private and public sector banks. The study concluded that new private banks had more computerized branches in comparison with old private banks and public sector banks. They recommended that public sector banks should offer better customer service.

Selvaraj[3]**(2009)** conducted a study on total quality management in Indian commercial banks. Ex post facto research design was used in the study as many of the variables used in the study were used in previous studies. The study had a sample size of 300. The respondents were bank employees. The data were collected using a mail survey. A questionnaire was developed based on total service quality dimensions. The study found significant differences among public, private and foreign banks in their total quality of services. The study also found that foreign banks performed better in top management commitment, customer focus and Services cape. Private sector banks were found to have better service culture and human resource management. Public sector fared better in employee satisfaction.

Kallol Jitesh et al.[4]**(2009)** in their study entitled, "Customer Relationship Management (CRM) Best Practices and Customer Loyalty – A Study of Indian Retail Banking Sector", explored the association between development of customer relationship management (CRM) best practices and loyalty of profitable customers in Indian retail banking sector. The study comprises two parts. The first part called the CRM best practice survey involves the use of descriptive research design; the second part which is based on case study research involves the use of embedded customer loyalty survey. The result implies that going for CRM deployment may not be a profitable strategy for retail banks, particularly in the Indian banking.

---

[1] Solomon.E, p&p sec manager, (2007), " An Empirical Investigation to Job Characteristics and Org Climate", *Journal of Applied Psychology*, Vol.71, pp. 247-259.

[2] Hugar S.S. and Vaz N.H ,(2008), "An Evaluation of Customer Orientation of Indian Public Sector Banks", *Indian Journal of Marketing*, pp. 31-41.

[3] M. Selvaraj, (2009),"Total Quality Management in Indian Commercial Banks: A Comparative Study", *Journal of Marketing & Communication,*Vol.4, p. 59.

[4] Kallol Das, Jitesh Parmar and Vijay Kumar Sadanand,(2009), "Customer Relationship Management (CRM) best practices and customer loyality - a study of Indian retail banking sector", *European journal of social schemes Europe*, Vol.11, No.1, p. 8.

Jamal et al.[1] **(2002)** in their paper explored the causal relationship between service quality and customer satisfaction and further, investigated the role of customer expertise in enhancing overall customer satisfaction. Data were collected randomly from 200 customers visiting a specific branch of Abu Dhabi commercial bank of UAE through questionnaire. The study measured service quality through core, relational and tangible dimensions, customer satisfaction through multiple interactions between bank and customers and lastly, customer expertise was measured through product class expertise dimension. Multiple regression and Anova were used to analyse the gathered data. The study concluded that both core and relational dimensions of service quality are associated with customer satisfaction. Further, customer expertise is found to be negatively related with customer satisfaction, i.e., as level of customers" expertise goes up, their satisfaction with service provider comes down or decreases.

Bellou and Andronikidi[2] **(2008)** in their paper tried to examine the internal service quality and its implications within the banking sector in terms of front-line employee behaviour, which is critical for service quality provided and customer satisfaction. Further, this effect was examined both for publicly and privately held banks of Greek city. Data were collected via questionnaires, which were administered to 10 employees who were selected randomly from each branch of 16 banks. The researchers gathered 113 questionnaires, out of which 105 questionnaires were fully and correctly completed. Internal service quality, pro-social behaviour and sector were three measures used in the study, where internal service quality consisting of 24 items based on 7-point Likert scale pertaining to seven distinct dimensions (reliability, responsiveness, competence, communication, understanding, courtesy and access), was measured to investigate the extent to which employees believe that their bank offers internal services of high quality. Further, instrument developed by Bettencourt and Brown (1997) included 5 items for each of its dimensions (role-prescribed customer service, cooperation and extra role behaviour) to access the pro-social behaviour. Finally, employees were asked to indicate whether the bank is a public or a private. Step wise regression was applied to examine the impact of internal service quality on overall pro-social behaviour as well as its dimensions. The findings of the study indicate that competence, communication and understanding predict overall pro-social behaviour for the public sector while reliability and access for the private sector. Further, competence and communication impact extra role behaviour

---

[1] Jamal, Ahmad and Kamal Naser (2002), "Customer Satisfaction and Retail Banking: An Assessment of Some of the Key Antecedents of Customer Satisfaction in Retail Banking," *International Journal of Bank Marketing*, Vol.20, pp. 146-160.

[2] Bellou, Victoria and Andreas Andronikidis (2008), "The Impact of Internal Service Quality on Customer Service Behaviour," *International Journal of Quality and Reliability Management*, Vol.25 Issue 9, 943-954.

displayed by individuals employed in public sector banks while individuals employed in private sector banks are being influenced by competence and reliability. Finally, for role prescribed customer service, reliability and access have a significant effect on both sectors, but in case of public sector competence is also identified.

Methlie et al.[1] **(1999)** studied factors that keep online customers loyal towards their bank on the basis of the data collected from customers of three banks through questionnaire accessible on the home page of their bank. The respondents filled out the questionnaire on their computer screens and returned the same via internet. 7- point scale was used to measure various constructs, viz., search costs, satisfaction, switching costs, loyalty, brand reputation. The findings of the study indicate that customer satisfaction and brand reputation are two most important determinants for both affective loyalty and co negative loyalty.

Ehigie and Benjamin Osayawe[2] **(2006)** examined how customer expectations, perceived service quality and satisfaction predict customer loyalty among bank customers in Nigeria. The study was conducted both as qualitative and quantitative research. For the qualitative study, 38 professional post-graduate students were selected who owned savings, current and electronic accounts. Out of which 20 were engaged in in-depth interview while 18 participated in the focus group discussion. Further, for quantitative research, 247 respondents responded to questionnaire items. Items relating to customer's expectations, customer loyalty, customer satisfaction and perceived service quality were used in the questionnaire. A hierarchical regression analysis was used to test the significant relationship of customer loyalty, customer expectations, service quality perception and satisfaction. The results indicate that service quality and satisfaction are significant predictors of customer loyalty, but not customer expectations.

Molina et al.[3] **(2007)** presented a causal model identifying the relational benefits of customer satisfaction in retail banking. Convenience sampling method was used to collect data in 2004 from bank customers of the three large Spanish cities located in central Spain. Multiple-item measurement scale was used to design the questionnaire, which included questions regarding the different related benefits, customer satisfaction, the number and types of financial products acquired as well as the length, continuity and degree of relationship with

---

[1] Methlie, Leif B. and Herbjorn Nysveen (1999), "Loyalty of Online Bank Customers," *Journal of Information Technology*, Vol.14, Issue (4), pp. 375-386.

[2] Ehigie and Benjamin Osayawe (2006), "Correlates of Customer Loyalty to their Bank: A Case Study in Nigeria," *International Journal of Bank Marketing*, Vol.24, Issue (7), pp. 494-508.

[3] Molina, Arturo, David Martin-Consuegra, and Agueda Esteban (2007), "Relational Benefits and Customer Satisfaction in Retail Banking," *International Journal of Bank Marketing*, Vol.25, Issue (4), pp. 253-271.

the financial entity. 14 items pertaining to different related benefits based on 7-point Likert scale were adapted from the study.

Hoq et al.[1](2010) examined the role of customer satisfaction in enhancing customer loyalty for Muslim and non-Muslim customers and the effects of customer loyalty on customers "Behavioural decisions in the Malaysian Islamic banking industry. Quota sampling was used for the study and 440 questionnaires were received. Seven point Likert scale was used to measure customer loyalty by adapting scale items. To test the reliability of customer satisfaction, customer loyalty, and intention to switch instruments, the Cronbach's alpha coefficient was computed.

The coefficient alpha exceeded the minimum standard of 0.70, which indicates that it provides a good estimate of internal consistency or reliability. The result shows that customer satisfaction is the most important driver to enhance customer loyalty for non-Muslim than Muslim customers. Further, result also implies that higher customer satisfaction leads to lower customer intention to switch a bank.

Rahman[2](2005) analysed customer experience management of an Indian bank. In this study brand loyalty of customers and employees were studied towards Punjab National Bank. Descriptive research design was used to gain insight into the current level of customer satisfaction with the banks, by rating the bank's interfaces such as employees and ATM (Automated Teller Machines) services on cognition, physical appearance, emotion and connectedness. The study had a sample size of 100 who were bank customers and convenient sampling was used to collect data. The study also conducted an employee survey to understand their level of satisfaction. Descriptive research design was used and the sample size was 21. The study concluded that, on average, a majority of customers were satisfied with the present functioning of the bank but would definitely be delighted if the bank changed its interface with the customers to become more cognitive (intelligent), emotional, physically pleasing and well connected. The loyalty of most of the bank employees was found be very good. Small sample size was a limitation of this study.

An overview of the studies reviewed shows that the present study differs from other earlier studies in the aspect of area of the study, period of the study, methodology, scope, tools and objectives. Hence, the present is an attempt to fill the research gap.

---

[1] Hoq, Mohammad Ziaul and Muslim Amin (2010), "The Role of Customer Satisfaction to Enhance Customer Loyalty," *African Journal of Business Management*, Vol.4, Issue (12), pp. 2385-2392.

[2] Rahmath Safeena and Hema Dale Abdullah (2011), Customer Perspectives on E- Business Value: Case Study on Internet Banking, *Journal of Internet Banking and Commerce*, Vol.15 Issue (1), pp. 1-13.

1.4. Importance of the Study

The banking business in India is witnessing high competition among private, public, foreign and co-operative sector players. Marketing of their services to end customers have been extremely challenging for the banks in such a highly competitive situation. Branding offers differentiation to banks when faced with competition. Branding can really create value like increasing more Adaptability, uniqueness, recognition etc.

1.5. Scope of the Study

The new edge Indian private banks like ICICI, HDFC, CUB etc., are growing faster compared to their public sector counterparts like SBI, BOB etc., The present study is titled 'Brand Management in Commercial Banks: A study in Erode district of Tamil Nadu'. The study focuses on various aspects of customer perception, level of attitude, customers' over all expectations and satisfaction about Brand Management in the study area. There are 39 banks in erode district of which 21 banks were public sector banks, 15 private sector banks and remaining constitute other banks. Six leading banks, two from public sector banks (State Bank of India and Bank of Baroda) and four from private sector banks (HDFC, Axis, CUB and ICICI) have been selected for the study.

1.6. Objectives of the Study

The objectives of the study are as follows:

1. To study the progress and development of brand management in commercial banks.
2. To study the customers' perception about brand management in selected commercial banks.
3. To study the customers' attitude towards brand management in selected commercial banks.
4. To measure the customer satisfaction among brand management in commercial banks.

1.7. Hypotheses of the Study

On the basis of the framed objectives, review of various studies, outcome of the pilot study, the researcher's theoretical knowledge, discussion and deliberations with experts the following null hypotheses have been framed and the same have been tested with various appropriate statistical tools.

H_{01}: There is no significant association between the personal variables of respondents (Age, Gender, Educational Qualification, Marital status, Main occupation, Annual income, Bank's branch, Average annual balance and Total experience with this bank) and their perception about brand management in commercial banks.

H_{02}: There is no significant association between the personal variables of respondents (Age, Gender, Educational Qualification, Marital status, Main occupation, Annual income, Bank's branch, Average annual balance and Total experience with this bank) and their attitude towards brand management in commercial banks.

H_{03}: There is no significant association between the personal variables of respondents (Age, Gender, Educational Qualification, Marital status, Main occupation, Annual income, Bank's branch, Average annual balance and Total experience with this bank) and their satisfaction on brand management in commercial banks.

1.8. Pilot Study and Pre-Testing

A pilot study was conducted during 2014. In the pilot study, questionnaires were presented and necessary modifications were carried out before being used for the final survey. A pilot study was conducted among sixty customers (20 from public sector banks and 40 from private sector banks). Based on the results of the study and personal observation, the requisite factors were identified to know the attitude of customers.

1.9. Period of the Study

The primary data for the present study were collected from July 2015 to December 2015. The secondary data pertaining to the study were reviewed up to December 2016.

1.10. Data Collection

The validity of any research is based on the systematic method of data collection and analysis. The study is based on both primary and secondary data. The primary data were collected from the respondents by using well structured questionnaires. The required primary data were collected from 580 sample respondents.

1.11. Sampling Scheme

Erode district occupies an important position both in industrial and agricultural aspects. Hence, for the present study Erode district has been purposively selected. There are 39 Banks functioning in Erode District as on March 2014, of these 21 are Public Sector banks and 15 are Private Sector banks. Another three Banks are Erode district central cooperation Bank Ltd

(EDCC), Tamil Nadu Industrial Investment corporation (TIIC), Pallavan grama bank. Totally, Public Sector banks have 171 branches and Private Sector Banks have 92 branches. In order to collect primary data for the purpose of the study, Multi Stage Sampling Technique was adopted.

On the basis of the list prepared by the RBI in 2014, the topmost 6 banks viz., have been selected. A sample of six banks (Two Public and Four Private Sector Banks) were selected at random from the broad categories of banks. Five branches from each bank were selected on convenience basis. From each branch twenty customers were selected and each bank has hundred sample customers. Hence, Two hundred sample customers from Public Sector banks and Four hundred sample customers from Private Sector banks were selected. Totally, Six hundred customer were selected from both Public and Private sector Banks.

Table 1.1: Distribution of Branch wise Sample Respondents

S.No	Name of the Bank (Public & Private)	Number of Branches Available	Number of Branches selected for the Study	Number of Samples selected Bankwise	Total Number of Samples selected Bankwise	Total Number of Samples selected Sectorwise
1	SBI	43	5	20	100	200
2	BOB	13	5	20	100	
3	AXIS	15	5	20	100	400
4	ICICI	12	5	20	100	
5	CUB	12	5	20	100	
6	HDFC	6	5	20	100	
Total					600	600

Table 1.2 shows the number of questionnaires issued and number of questionnaires received from the customers of the six banks in Erode district.

Table 1.2: Response Rate of Questionnaire

Banks	Distributed	Used	Total
SBI	100	99	196
BOB	100	97	
AXIS	100	97	384
ICICI	100	95	
CUB	100	97	
HDFC	100	95	
Total			580

Out of 600 Questionnaires distributed to the customers, 590 completed questionnaires were received. Owing to illegible handwriting, incomplete entries and inconsistency in the questionnaires from the respondents, 580 sample customers were considered for final analysis.

The secondary data were collected from the Journals, Books, Websites and Libraries.

1.12. Data Processing and Analysis

The filled up questionnaires were thoroughly checked to ensure accuracy, consistency and completeness. The collected data were scrutinized, edited and tabulated. For the analysis of the data, statistical tools like Chi-square test, f- test (Anova), Z- test , Multiple Regression Analysis, Cronbach's Alpha's Reliability Analysis, Factor Analysis and Garrett Ranking techniques have been applied. The well known statistical package SPSS 11.0 was employed.

1.13. Operational Definition

1.13.1. Commercial Banks

The financial institutions which accept deposits for various terms like savings, current, recurring and fixed; facilitates money market transactions and provides various financial services like lending loans to general public, factoring etc.,

1.13.2. Public Sector Banks

The banks in which government holds at least 51 percent of its own stake in equity share capital and the remaining stake might be issued to the general public. Some of the examples are SBI, BOB etc.

1.13.3. Private Sector Banks

The banks in which government has no stake equity share capital but controls its activities through RBI. Some of the example are ICICI, HDFC, CUB, AXIS etc.

1.13.4. Customer

The term refers to the individual who have dealings with the banks either by way of having an account in the form of a deposit or by way of availing of a loan facility or both.

1.13.5. Brand

A brand is a symbol, a word, a letter or a combination of them all which helps the customer identify the product or service of the banks.

1.13.6. Customer Perception

Customer Perception refers to the process, by which a customer selects, organizes and interprets information/stimuli inputs to create a meaningful picture of the brand or the product of the banks.

1.13.7. Customer Attitude

Customer's attitude simply as a composite of a customer's beliefs, feelings and behavioural intention towards some object within the context of marketing. A customer can hold negative or positive beliefs or feelings toward a product or service. A behavioural intention is defined by the consumer's belief or feeling with respect to the product or service of the banks.

1.13.8. Customer Satisfaction

Favorable opinion of the customer towards the services offered by the banks. The fulfillment of the expectations of customer regarding the services provided by the banks.

1.14. Limitations of the Study

The study has the following limitations

1) The sample size of the study is restricted to 580. Besides, the study was confined to Erode district only.
2) The findings of the study are confined to the period of study only, because customer expectations of the service as well as type of service provided by banks change from time to time. Therefore, the findings of the study indicate only contemporary views of the customers and may not hold good for all times to come.
3) This study covers only public and private sector banks in the study area. This excludes co operative banks and foreign banks.

1.15. Chapterisation Scheme

The present study has been presented in six chapters. They are as given below

Chapter I

Introduction and Design of the Study

Introduction , Statement of the problem, Review of literature, Importance of the Study, Scope of the Study, Objectives of the Study, Hypotheses, Methodology, Data processing and analysis, Limitations and Chapterisation scheme are discussed in the first chapter.

Chapter II

Commercial Banks and Brand Management : An Overview

This chapter reviews the various products and services provided by public and private sector bank to its customer.

Chapter III

Customers' Perception on Brand Management in Commercial Banks

This chapter presents the customers' perception towards brand management in commercial banks.

Chapter IV

Customers' Attitude towards Brand Management in Commercial Banks

In this chapter, an attempt is made to measure and analyse the customers' attitude towards brand management in commercial banks.

Chapter V

Customers' Satisfaction towards Brand Management in Commercial Banks

In this chapter, an attempt is made to ascertain and analyse collectively the level of customers' satisfaction of commercial banks in erode district.

Chapter VI

Summary of Findings, Suggestions and Conclusion

The last chapter deals with the sum of the findings that emerged from the analyses and offers necessary suggestions for improving the perception, attitude and satisfaction level of customers in commercial banks. This chapter ends with a suitable conclusion.

CHAPTER II

COMMERCIAL BANKS AND BRAND MANAGEMENT: AN OVERVIEW

2.1. Introduction

Banking institutions offer a collection of services from deposits in savings accounts to housing and business loans to cheque clearing, underwriting and credit cards. The fastest changes in the world and the technological advances in globalization are changing banking backgrounds. Individuals and business customers are demanding fast and new products and services. The banking industry is also highly integrated and has its own share of challenges to provide financial objectives to the people and organizations. Different banking companies operate their activities differently. Hence the banks can be classified in a diversity of ways, according to applicable law and regulations, based on their domicile, on basis of ownership, on basis of function and structure.

Commercial Banks Structure

Commercial Banks	Public Sector Banks	SBI & Associates
		Other Nationalized Banks
		Other Public Sector Banks
	Private Sector Banks	Old Private Sector Banks
		New Private Sector Banks
	Foreign Banks	
	Regional Rural Banks	

2.2. Commercial Banks

Banking means accepting deposits of money from the public for the purpose of lending or investment. Deposit-taking institutions take the form of commercial banks, when they use the deposits for making commercial, real estate and other loans. Commercial banks are acting as financial intermediaries, raising funds from depositors and lending the same funds to borrowers. The commercial bank serves the interests of its depositors by utilising the funds collected in profitable ventures and in-return offers variety of services to its customers. Services provided by commercial banks include, credit and debit cards, bank accounts, deposits and loans, and deposit mobilization. They also provide secured and unsecured loans. These commercial banks are the oldest institutions in banking history and generally have a wide network of branches spread throughout the area of their operations. Commercial banks may either be owned by the government or may be run in the private sector. Based on their ownership structure they can be classified as:

2.2.1. *Public Sector Banks*

Public sectors banks are those banks in which the government has a major stake and they usually need to emphasis on social objectives than on profitability. The main objectives of public sector banks are to ensure that there is no monopoly control of banking and financial services by few individuals or business houses and to ensure compliance with regulations and promote the needs of the underprivileged and weaker sections of society, cater to the needs of agriculture and other priority sectors and prevent concentration of wealth and economic power. These banks, in particular, have a revolutionary role in lending to priority sector, credit to agriculture, small businesses and small businesses. In India, there are 27 public sector banks nationalized by the government to protect the interests of the common people. Public sector banks can be further classified as:

Nationalized Banks

After independence, there were many banks in private banks. At that time, private banks often focus on providing financial services. Indian banking industry has become an important instrument for the growth of Indian economy in the 1960s. At the same time, it has emerged as a major employer and has confirmed a debate about the possibility of nationalization of bank affairs. From the midnight of July 1969, the Indian government issued a mandate and nationalized 14 big business banks. Within two weeks of the Ordinance affair the Parliament passed the Banking Companies (Acquisition and Delivery) Act. On August 9, 1969, the president accepted the approval. Six more banks were nationalised in 1980. The reason for nationalization is to provide more control of the government to credit. The second step of nationalization was the 91% circular in banking business in India.

Other Public Sector Banks

There are 27 Public sector banks in India which includes 19 nationalised banks, 6 SBI and its association and 2 other public sector banks.

2.2.2. *Private Sector Banks*

The private-sector banks are banks where majority of their ownership is held by private shareholders and not by the government. Private sector banks are owned, managed and controlled by private investors and are free to operate within the market forces. Ensuring their safety and smooth functions are usually regulatory criteria such as entry barriers and minimum net worth. The security of public deposits entrusted with such companies confirms and is regularly arranged by the guidelines provided by the RBI. ICICI Bank, Yes Bank and Axis

Bank are some examples of private banks in India. Private sector banks in India can be classified as private Indian banks and private foreign banks. Private Indian banks can also be classified as old private banks and new private sector banks.

Old Private Sector Banks

Not all private sector banks were nationalised in 1969, and 1980. The private banks which were not nationalised are collectively known as the old private sector banks and include banks such as The Jammu and Kashmir Bank Ltd., Lord Krishna Bank Ltd etc.

New Private Sector Banks

Entry of private sector banks was however prohibited during the post-nationalisation period. In July 1993, as part of the banking improvement process and as determine to induce competition in the banking sectors, RBI permitted the private sector to enter into the banking system. This resulted in the creation of a new set of private sector banks, which are jointly known as the new private sector banks. As at end March, 2009 there were 7 new private sector banks and 15 old private sector banks operating in India.

2.2.3. Foreign Banks

Foreign banks have their registered and head offices in a foreign country but operate their branches in India. The RBI permits these banks to operate either through branches or through wholly-owned subsidiaries. The main activity of most foreign banks in India has been in the corporate segment. However, some of the superior foreign banks have also made consumer financing a significant part of their portfolios. These banks offer products such as automobile finance, home loans, credit cards, household consumer finance etc. Foreign banks in India are required to adhere to all banking regulations, including priority-sector lending norms as applicable to domestic banks. In addition to the entry of the new private banks in the mid-90s, the increased presence of foreign banks in India has also contributed to boosting competition in the banking sector.

2.2.4. Regional Rural Banks

On second October 1975, the Indian government set up regional rural banks (RRBs). These are banking companies operating in various states of India. They have been created to serve the rural areas with banking and financial services. These banks support small and marginal farmers through lending in rural areas. They meet the credit needs of small and marginal farmers, agricultural workers, artisans and small entrepreneurs. RRB's plans are generally offered by scheduled banks, usually a nationalized commercial bank. Each RRB is an institution funded by the state government and the public sector bank with the central government. However, the RRP's urban activities can be set up and their area may be urban areas. They are also called Grameen Banks/Gramin Banks. Over the years, the government has introduced several measures to increase the viability and profitability of the RRPs. One of these is a amalgamation of RRPs of the bank with the same incentive within a state. Compared to 196 at the end of March 2005, this process has increased the number of RRBs to 56.

2.2.5. *Profile of the Selected Private Sector Banks and Public Sector Banks*

A brief description of the various services rendered by the selected private and public sector banks is given below.

Private Sector Banks

HDFC Bank[1]

HDFC Bank Ltd is a commercial bank of India, incorporated in August 1994, after the Reserve Bank of India allowed establishing private sector banks. This bank was promoted by the Housing Development Finance Corporation (Housing Finance Corporation), India's premier housing finance company (established in 1997). HDFC Bank has 1,412 branches and 3,295 ATMs in 528 cities in India. All branches of the bank are connected directly online. As of September 30, 2008, the total assets of the bank stood at 1006.82 billion. In the financial year 2008-09, the net profit of the bank stood at Rs.2,244.9 crore and 41% in the previous fiscal. The Bank's annual revenue increased to Rs 19,622.8 crore in 2008-09, up by 58%.June, 2017 Net Profit - 14,550 crore. An increase of 18.3% compared to the previous year. Balance Sheet Size- 863,840 crore.

HDFC bank is one of the big banks of India, along with State Bank of India, ICICI bank and Axis bank –its main competitors. The short history of HDFC bank is as follows:

Business Focus

HDFC Bank is linked to three major business sectors–Wholesale banking S\services, Retail banking services and Treasuries. It has entered the banking consortia of over 50 corporate for providing working capital finance, trade services, corporate finance and merchant banking. It provides sophisticated production structures in foreign exchange and shares, money market and dept trading and equity research

---

[1]http:// www.Money control.com/stocks/company_info/company_history.php?sc_did=HDF01

Wholesale Banking Services

The bank's target market ranges from large blue- chip manufacturing companies in the Indian corporations to small and mid-sized corporate and agri-based businesses. For these customer, the bank provides a wide range of commercial and transactional banking services, including working capital finance, trade services, transactional services, cash management etc.. The bank is also a leading provider of structured solutions, which combine cash management services with vendor and distributor finance for facilitating superior supply chain management for its corporate customers. HDFC Bank has made significant inroads into the banking consortia of a number of leading Indian corporate including multinationals, companies from the domestic business houses and prime public sector companies. It is recognized as a leading provider of cash management and transactional banking solutions to corporate customers, mutual funds, stock exchange members and banks.

Retail Banking Services

The objective of the Retail bank is to offer its target market customers a complete range of financial products and services, giving the customer a one–stop window for all banking necessities. The products are backed by outstanding service and delivered to customers through the increasing branch network, as well as through another delivery channels like ATMs, phone banking, net banking and mobile banking. HDFC bank was the first bank in India to start an international debit card in association with VISA Electron and issue the Mastercard and Maestro debit cards. The bank launched its credit card business in late 2001. By March 2014, the bank had a total card base of over 19 million. The bank is also one of the top players in the "merchant acquiring" business with over 70,000 point-of-sale terminals for debit/credit cards acceptance at merchant establishments. The bank is well positioned as a leader in various net based B2C opportunities including a wide range of internet banking service for fixed deposits, loans, bill payments etc.,

Treasury

Within this business, the bank has three main product parts, foreign currency and derivatives, local currency markets and bonds, and equities. These services are provided by the Bank's Treasury Committee. Depending on the legal reserve requirements, deposits of 25% of bank securities should be kept. Treasury business is responsible for managing the income and market risk in this investment segment.

Logo and Slogan

- To provide attractive financial services for housing as per the national target of decent housing for all. In February 2000, the times group was merged with HDFC, and in May 2008, HFC with the Punjab Centurion Bank.
- HDFC logo is a perfect blend of focus, over whelming and proving complete security and deep meaning make this logo stands apart in finance logos.
- The four from open gateways on each side gives impression of welcoming customers from all ways and provide them all kind of services at a single place.

Slogan: We understand your world.

ICICI Bank[2]

Since 1955, the Industrial credit and investment corporation of India limited was incorporated at the initiative of world Bank, the government of India and representative of Indian industry, with the aim of creating a development financial institution for providing medium-term and long-term project financing to Indian business. In 1994, ICICI established Banking Corporation as a banking subsidiary. Formerly known as industrial credit and investment corporation of India, ICICI banking corporation was later renamed as 'ICICI Bank Limited'. ICICI founded a separate legal entity, ICICI Bank, to undertake normal banking operations. In 2001, ICICI acquired Bank of Madura.

After receiving all necessary regulatory approvals, ICICI integrated the group's financing and banking operations, both wholesale and retail, into a single entity.

ICICI Bank is India's second largest bank with total assets of Rs4,736.47 billion at March31, 2012 and profit after tax Rs 64.65 billion for the year ended march 31, 2012. The bank has a network of 2,768 branches and 9,363 ATMs in India and has a presence in 19 countries including India. ICICI Bank offers a wide range of banking products and financial services to corporate and retail customers through a variety of delivery channels and through its specialized subsidiaries in the areas of investment banking, life and non-life insurance, venture capital and asset management. The bank currently has subsidiaries in the United Kingdom, Russia and Canada, branches in United States, Singapore, Bahrain, Hong Kong, Sri Lanka, Qatar and Dubai. International finance centre and representative offices in United Arab Emirates, China, South Africa, Bangladesh, Thailand, Malaysia and Indonesia. Its UK subsidiary has

---

[2] http:// www.iloveindia.com/finance/bank/private banks/icici_bank.html

established branches in Belgium and Germany. ICICI Bank's equity shares are listed in India on Bombay Stock Exchange and the National Stock Exchange of India limited and its American depositary receipts are listed on the New York Stock Exchange.189% increase in standalone profit after tax from Rs. 702 crore (US$ 108 million) for the quarter ended March 31, 2016 (Q4-2016) to Rs. 2,025 crore (US$ 312 million) for the quarter ended March 31, 2017 (Q4-2017).14% year-on-year growth in domestic advances; retail portfolio grew by 19% year-on-year and constituted 52% of the total portfolio at March 31, 2017.

Symbol and Logo

The corporate identity of a company can truly be said to be a symbol of the values that the company stands for.

- The logo depicts a dynamic individual with drive and conviction and personifies the human capital of this company, which is indispensable to further progress.
- The individual in the logo also symbolizes the strong human focus of the group. Whether, in the form of reaching out to a shareholder or individual customers.
- The 'I' in the logo also stands for 'Numero Uno', a position that the group has always strived to achieve. It also lends itself to representing the 'ICICI' name.

The corporate colours reflect ICICI group's core values.

- Orange – "Thecolour of Dynamism".
  A company that responds to market conditions and customer needs. Breaking new standards in financial and banking solutions
- Blue – "The colour of Trust and Depth".
  Trust brought about by the security of knowing that dealing with an organization that brings to expert knowledge, a high level of commitment, professionalism and ethics.
- Maroon – "The colour of Warmth".
  An organization that goes beyond the basics to understand its customer and provide them with products and services with a view to building lasting relationship.

Brand Strategy

2001: Safer, Simpler and Smarter.

2003: Hum Hai Na.

2005: Opportunities Unlimited

2008: Power of Belief

AXIS Bank[3]

Axis bank was formed as UTI when it was incorporated in 1994 when government of India allowed private players in the banking sectors. The bank has a large footprint of 3,304 domestic branches (including extension counters) and 14,163 ATMs across the country as on 31st March 2017. The overseas operations of the Bank are spread over nine international offices with branches at Singapore, Hong Kong, Dubai (at the DIFC), Colombo and Shanghai; representative offices at Dhaka, Dubai, Abu Dhabi and an overseas subsidiary at London, UK. The International offices focus on corporate lending, trade finance, syndication, investment banking and liability businesses.

Axis Bank is one of the first new generation private sector banks to have begun operations in 1994. The Bank was promoted in 1993, jointly by Specified Undertaking of Unit Trust of India (SUUTI) (then known as Unit Trust of India), Life Insurance Corporation of India (LIC), General Insurance Corporation of India (GIC), National Insurance Company Ltd., The New India Assurance Company Ltd.,. The Oriental Insurance Company Ltd. and United India Insurance Company Ltd. The share holding of Unit Trust of India was subsequently transferred to SUUTI, an entity established in 2003.With a balance sheet size of Rs. 6,01,468 crores as on 31st March 2017, Axis Bank has achieved consistent growth and with a 5 year CAGR (2011-12 to 2016-17) with 16% in Total Assets, 13% in Total Deposits, 17% in Total Advances.

Branches and Business

Set up with a capital of Rs. 115 crores- with UTI contributing Rs 100 crores, LIC contributing Rs 7.5 crores and its four subsidiaries contributing Rs.1.5 crores, the bank came in operation with its first registered office at Ahmadabad. Today, Axis bank has more than 726 branch offices and extension counters spread over 341 cities, towns and villages of the country.

Presently, the authorized share capital of Axis bank is Rs 300 crores and the paid up share capital is Rs 232.86 crores. The Axis bank is currently capitalized with Rs. 282.65 crores with a public holding of 57.05% apart from the promoters.

---

[3] http://en.wikipedia.org/wiki/Axis_bank

Facilities and Services

The Axis bank has been provided special facilities and services to the customers. In detailed have been given below:

Corporate Facilities

- Cash Credit
- Working Capital Demand Loan
- Export Finance
- Short Term Loan
- Term Loan
- Clean Bill Discounting
- LC Backed Bill Discounting
- Co-acceptance of Bills
- Credit Facilities against Guarantee or Stand by Letter of Credit issued by Foreign bank
- Letter of Credit
- Bank Guarantee and
- Solvency Certificates

Personal Facilities

- Home Loans
- Personal Loans
- Car Loan
- Zero Balance Saving Accounts
- VBV - Online purchases using Credit Card
- VBV / MSC – Online purchases using Debit Card
- Mobile Banking
- NRI Account
- Study Loans
- Gold and
- Easy Saving Account

Symbol and Slogan

Having successfully established itself as a customer-centric bank, Axis Bank has taken a leap towards a fresh stance. The private sector bank has recently launched a new brand campaign to shift its positioning statement from 'Aapka Solution'to 'Badhti Ka Naam Zindagi'.

"The repositioning of Axis Bank from *'Aapka Solution'* to *'BADHTI KA NAAM ZINDAGI'* is an important milestone in the journey of Axis Bank brand. The new campaign marks the evolution of Axis Bank brand from playing the role of a 'problem solver' in the customers life, to that of an 'encouraging and enthusing partner' by owning an attitude and belief that resonates with target audience in everyday life".

Slogan: Badhti ka naam zindagi

City Union Bank[4]

The Kumbakonam bank Ltd as it was then called was incorporated as a limited company on 31st October 1904. The first Memorandum of Association was signed by twenty devoted and prominent citizens of Kumbakonam including Sarvashri R. Santhanam Iyer, S.Krishna Iyer, V.Krishnaswami Iyengar and T.S.Raghavachariar.

T.S. Raghavachariar was the First Agent of the Bank.In 1908, he was succeeded by Shri R. Santhanam Iyer who became the Secretary of the bank under the amended Articles of Association which created the office of a Secretary to be in charge of the Banks' Management in the place of the Agent, which post he held till his death in 1926. He was succeeded by Shri. S. Mahalinga Iyer as Secretary who subsequently became the First full-time Managing Director of the bank in tune with the amendment of Articles in 1929.He held the position of Secretary from 1926 to 1929 and the Managing Director from 1929 to 1963.

The bank in the launch preferred the role of a regional bank and slowly but steadily built for itself a place in (Delta District) Thanjavur. The first Branch of the Bank was opened at Mannargudi on 24th January 1930.Thereafter, branches were opened at Nagapattinam, Sannanallur, Ayyampet, Tirukattupalli, Tiruvarur, Manapparai, Mayuram and Porayar within a span of twenty five years. The Bank was included in the Second Schedule of Reserve Bank of India Act 1934, on 22nd March 1945.

The Bank celebrated its Golden Jubilee on 14th November 1954 at Kumbakonam under the President ship of Shri.C.R.Srinivasan, Editor& Director, Reserve Bank of India.

In 1957, the bank took over the assets and liabilities of the Common Wealth Bank Limited and in the process annexed to it the five Branches of Common Wealth Bank Limited at Aduthurai, Kodavasal, Valangaiman, Jayankondacholopuram and Ariyalur.

---

[4] http://www.iloveindia.com/finance/bank/private banks/city-union-bank.html

In 1963,Shri. R. A.Venkataramani Iyer took charge as the Chairman of the Bank which position he held up to 1969.

The Tamil Nadu-based bank had registered a net profit of Rs. 83.34 crores, City Union Bank said in a BSE filing.

Private sector lender City Union Bank on Feb11, 2016 and 10 % rise in net profit isRs. 113.05crores for the third quarter ended Dec 3, 2016.

Products and Services

Personal Banking– "Under this City Union Bank offers wide range of products and services such as saving accounts, deposit scheme, home loans, education loans, debit card and many more".

NRI banking–" It offers products and services such as deposits, remittance and other services such as providing PAN assistance and lockers services".

Public Sector Banks

State Bank of India[5]

The progress of State Bank of India can be traced back to the first decade of the 19th century. It began with the establishment of the Bank of Calcutta in Calcutta, on 2, June 1806. The bank was redesigned as the Bank of Bengal, three years later, on 2 January 1809. It was the first ever joint-stock bank of the British India, established under the sponsorship of the Government of Bengal. Subsequently, the Bank of Bombay (established on 15, April 1840) and the Bank of Madras (established on 1 July 1843). These three banks dominated the modern banking scenario in India, until when they were amalgamated to form the Imperial Bank of India, on 27, Jan 1921.

An important turning point in the history of State Bank of India is the launch of the first Five Year Plan of independent India, in 1951. The Plan aimed at serving the Indian economy in general and the rural sector of the country, in particular. Until the Plan, the commercial banks of the country, including the Imperial Bank of India, confined their services to the urban sector. Moreover, they were not equipped to respond to the growing needs of the economic revival taking shape in the rural areas of the country. Therefore, in order to serve the economy as a whole and rural sector in particular, the All India Rural Credit Survey Committee recommended the formation of a state-partnered and state-sponsored bank.

---

[5] http://www.iloveindia.com/finance/bank/nationalised-banks/state-bank-of-india.html

The all India Rural Credit Survey Committee proposed the takeover of the Imperial Bank of India and integrating with it, the former state-owned or state-associate banks. Subsequently, an Act was passed in the Indian Parliament onMay 1955. As a result, the State Bank of India (SBI) was established on 1 July 1955. This resulted in making the State Bank of India more powerful, because as much as a quarter of the resources of the Indian banking system were controlled directly by the State. Later on, the State Bank of India (Subsidiary Banks) Act was passed in 1959. The Act enabled the State Bank of India to make the eight former State-associate banks as its subsidiaries.

The State Bank of India emerged as a pacesetter, with its operations carried out by the 480 offices comprising branches, sub offices, three Local Head Offices and inherited from the Imperial Bank. Instead of serving as mere repositories of the community's savings and lending to creditworthy parties, the State Bank of India catered to the needs of the customers by banking purposefully. The bank served the heterogeneous financial needs of the planned economic development.

Branches

The corporate center of SBI is located in Mumbai. In order to cater to different functions, there are several other establishments in and outside Mumbai, apart from the corporate center. The bank boasts of having as many as 14 local head offices and 57 Zonal Offices located at major cities throughout India. It is recorded that SBI has about 10,000 branches, well networked to cater to its customers throughout India.

ATM-Services

SBI provides easy access to money to its customers through more than 8,500 ATMs in India. The Bank also facilitates the free transaction of money at the ATMs of State Bank Group, which includes the ATMs of State Bank of India as well as the Associate Banks – State Bank of Bikaner & Jaipur, State Bank of Hyderabad, State Bank of Indore, etc.,

Subsidiaries

The State Bank Group includes a network of eight banking subsidiaries and several non-banking subsidiaries. Through the establishments, it offers various services including merchant banking services, fund management, factoring services, primary dealership in government securities, credit cards and insurance.

The banking subsidiaries are

- State Bank of Bikaner and Jaipur (SBBJ)
- State Bank of Hyderabad (SBH)
- State Bank of Mysore (SBM)
- State Bank of Patiala (SBP)
- State Bank of Travancore (SBT)

Product and Services

Personal Banking

- SBI Term Deposits SBI Loan For Pensioners
- SBI Recurring Deposits Loan Against Mortgage of Property
- SBI Housing Loan, Loan Against Shares & Debentures
- SBI Car Loan Rent Plus Scheme and
- SBI Educational Loan Medi-Plus Scheme

Other Services

- Agriculture/Rural Banking
- NRI Services
- ATM Services
- Demat Services
- Corporate Banking
- Internet Banking
- Mobile Banking
- International Banking
- Safe Deposit Locker
- RBIEFT
- E-Pay
- E-Rail
- SBI Vishwayatra Foreign Travel Card
- Broking Services and
- Gift Cheques

Emblem

- The first emblem for the State Bank of India was adopted in '1955'.
- At present, " logo of Bank of India is a blue circle with a small cut at the bottom. It was designed by Shekhar Kamat, an alumni of National Institute of Design, Ahemedabad".
- "One of the concepts behind the design of this logo is that the big circle in blue reflects unity and completeness while the white one represents common man as a vital part of thebank, despite the huge size of the bank".
- "The logo also suggests a keyhole which is said to be the symbol of safety, security and strength".

Slogan: Pure banking, Nothing else.

Bank of Baroda[6]

Bank of Baroda (BoB) was founded by Maharaja Sayajirao Gaekwad in July 1908. It started with a paid up capital of Rs 10 lakhs. "Bank of Baroda is a pioneer in various customer centric initiatives in the Indian banking sector. Bank is amongst first in the industry to complete an all-inclusive rebranding exercise wherein various novel customer centric initiatives were undertaken along with the change of logo. The initiatives include setting up of specialized NRI Branches, Gen-Next Branches and Retail Loan Factories/ SME Loan Factories with an assembly line approach of processing loans for speedy disbursal of loans".

Ever since its rebranding in 2005, bank has consistently promoted its major strengths viz., large international presence; technological advancement and superior customer service etc.. Bank had introduced the sub brand BARODA NEXT–State of the Art–Straight from the Heart to showcase how it has utilized technology to nurture long term relationships for superior customer experience. The sub brand has been reinforced by alternate delivery channels such as internet banking, ATMs, Mobile banking etc., and robust delivery outfits like Retail Loan Factories, SME Loan Factories, City Sales Office etc. Bank as constant endeavor to strengthen its branch/ATM network combined with well informed staff offering personalized service at its various touch points have enhanced customer interactions and satisfaction. Thus the Bank has firmly positioned itself as a technologically advanced customer–centric bank.

---

[6] http://wapedia.mobi/en/bank_of_baroda

Bank of Baroda is the third largest public sector bank in India, after State Bank of India and Punjab national bank. BOB has total assets in excess of Rs 2.27 crores or Rs. 2,274 billion, a network of over 3,000 branches and offices, more than 1,100 ATMs. It offers a wide range of banking product and financial services to corporate and retail customer through a variety of delivery channels and through its specialized subsidiaries and affiliates in the area of investment banking, credit cards and asset management.

Maharajah of Baroda Sir Sayajirao Gaekwad III founded the bank on July 20, 1980 in the princely state of Baroda, in Gujarat. The bank, along with 13 other major commercial bank of India was nationalized on 19 July 1969by the government of India.

International Presence

In its international expansion Bank of Baroda followed the Indian Diaspora and especially that of the Gujarat. It has significant international presence with a network of 72 offices in 25 countries, six subsidiaries and four representative offices. Among Bank of Baroda's 42 overseas branches are ones in the world's major financial centers i.e. New York, London, Dubai, Hong Kong (which it has upgraded recently), Brussels and Singapore, as well as a number in other countries. The bank is engaged in retail banking via 17 branches of subsidiaries in Botswana, Guyana, Kenya, Tanzania, and Uganda. Bank of Baroda also has a Joint-Venture Bank in Zambia with nine branches. Bank of Baroda maintains representative offices in Malaysia, china, Thailand, and Australia. It plans to upgrade its offices in China and Malaysia shortly to a branch and joint-venture, respectively.

"Bank of Baroda has received permission or in principle approval from host country regulators to open new offices in Trinidad and Tobago and Ghana, where it is seeking to establish joint ventures or subsidiaries. The bank has received Reserve Bank of India approval for operation in Bahrain, South Africa, Kuwait, Mozambique and Qater and is establishing offices in Canada, New Zealand, Sri Lanka, Bahrain, Saudi Arabia, and Russia. It also has plans to extend its existing operation in the United Kingdom, the United Arab Emirates, and Botswana".

Symbol

- Symbol is a unique representation of a universal symbol. It comprises dual "B" letter forms that hold the rays of the rising sun, namely "Baroda Sun".The sun is the excellent representation of what the Bank stands for. It is the single most powerful source of light and energy; its far reaching rays dispel darkness to illuminate everything they touch.

- The single colour, compelling vermillion palette has been chosen for its distinctiveness as it stands for hope and energy.

Slogan: India's international Bank.

2.3.   Branding

With a jump in the Indian economy from a manufacturing sector, that never really took off, to a nascent service sector, banking as a whole is undergoing a change. A great option for customers translates into large demands for financial products, customizing services faster than competitive advantage. The altering customer demographics compel to create a differentiated platform based on new technology, improved service and banking convenience.

Branding is the process of stamping a product with some identifiable name or mark or combination of both. A good brand agreement is memorable and desirable. If nobody remembers this, the brand is not useful and nobody is good if it does not like it. A good brand promises evokes feelings, because feelings drive actions and creating the promise means defining the brand. This promise is unique and must be uniquely identified with the company. In a industry, promises may be very close, but if the company has any hope of winning, it takes a very specific part of its commitment and is clear from the promises of other companies. Having the promises is to manage the ability. It refers to static actions with the ability to provide what it needs. It is reliable and compatible technology and systems. Brands are much more than names or logos. One way to do business with brands is because they are a reputation or a sign.

A good brand story tells the truth about a corporate fact. Successful brands include good stories. But it's a beginning. If the tag line does not match the staff behavior, the brand will have a great deal of services offered by a company. A brand stories can be used to further expand and deepen brand ideas with examples of man's concerns, aspirations, and emotions. Ideally, brand stories have captured the essence of the past and the future income. They help not only to customers but also to provide stimulus and direction for employees. An important aspect of the brand story is that it is consistent with everything the company does. A product may die but well maintained brand never dies.

In the present scenario, the expectations of the customers are different. Their expectations are dynamic. The bankers cannot fulfill the customer expectations of all their customers. According to customer point of view, their fulfillment expectations becomes first preferences and unfulfilled expectations becomes low level ranking. The collected primary data have been analysed with the help of Garrett's Ranking Techniques.

2.3.1. Bank Brand at the Top of the Mind of Customers

The study made an attempt to find which bank's brands is in the top of the mind of customers. It is found the 'SBI' scores the highest followed by CUB, Indian bank, Canara bank, IOB, ICICI, KVB, HDFC.

Table 2.1: Bank Brands at the Top of the Mind of Customers

Banks	Total Score	Mean Score	Rank
Canara Bank	2003	3.45	4
KVB	1567	2.70	7
Indian Bank	2010	3.46	3
CUB	2156	3.71	2
Axis	1267	2.18	10
ICICI	1659	2.86	6
SBI	2237	3.86	1
BOI	1314	2.27	9
IOB	1993	3.43	5
BOB	1218	2.1	11
HDFC	1484	2.56	8

Table 2.2: Bank Brands at the Top of the Mind of Customer (Private Sector& Public Sector)

Bank (private sector)	Total Score	Mean Score	Rank
CUB	2156	3.71	1
ICICI	1659	2.86	2
KVB	1567	2.70	3
HDFC	1484	2.56	4
Axis	1267	2.18	5
Bank (public sector)	**Total Score**	**Mean Score**	**Rank**
SBI	2237	3.86	1
Indian Bank	2010	3.46	2
Canara Bank	2003	3.45	3
IOB	1993	3.43	4
BOI	1314	2.27	5
BOB	1218	2.1	6

With regard to bank brands at the top of the mind among customers, SBI ranked first with the highest score of 2237 out of the selected sample banks. The second and third place go to CUB and Indian bank with the score of 2156 and 2010 respectively.

It is evident from the Table 2.2, in the private sector group, CUB ranked first with the highest score of 2156 and ICICI scored 1659 and got second position which clearly brings out the important place and brand power in the minds of customers. In public sector group, SBI and Indian banks hold the first and second ranks.

2.3.2. *Identification of Brand Logos of Banks*

A logo says a lot about the bank itself. The logo has come to acquire so much importance in the branding exercise of the banks that many have changed the logo to suit the communication needs.

Table 2.3: Sector Wise Bank Logos Identification

Public sector bank brand	Logo	Total score	Mean Score	Rank
SBI	State Bank of India	1580	2.72	1
BOB	Bank of Baroda	1573	2.71	2
Private sector bank brand	Logo	Total score	Mean Score	Rank
ICICI	ICICI Bank	1520	2.26	1
AXIS	AXIS BANK	1505	2.59	2
CUB	CITY UNION BANK LTD	1498	2.58	3
HDFC	HDFC BANK	1493	2.57	4

Table 2.3 displays logos of the several banks which are used to identify the brands. In the public sector category SBI and Bank of Baroda stood first and second places with scores of 1580 and 1573 respectively. In the private sector category, in terms logo identification ICICI bank ranked first with the highest score of 1520 and AXIS bank ranked second with the score of 1505.

2.3.3. *Advertisement Media of Banks*

Advertising plays an important role in introducing various products to customers. Many media are also available to offer advertisements like TV, magazines, news papers etc. An attempt is made to find how the customers come to know about the banks.

Table 2.4: Media of Advertisement

Sources	Private	Public	Total
News papers	40(83.3%)	8(16.7%)	48(100%)
Magazines	76(75.2%)	25(24.8%)	101(100%)
Television	71(80.7%)	17(19.3%)	88(100%)
Wall painting	41(54.7%)	34(45.3%)	75(100%)
Hoardings/Banners	51(67.1%)	25(32.9%)	76(100%)
SMS	27(56.2%)	21(43.8%)	48(100%)
Bus paintings	5(25.0%)	15(75.0%)	20(100%)
Internet/Web	73(58.9%)	51(41.1%)	124(100%)
Total	384(66.2%)	196(33.8%)	580(100.0%)

From the table 2.4, it is clear that 83.3% of customers got the knowledge about private sector banks through newspapers and in case of public sector banks 75% of the customers got knowledge about bank through bus painting.

2.3.4. *Knowledge About Slogan (Punch Line)*

The banks across the world use small phrase tagline as punch lines to convey the main objective and purpose of the banks. These are easy to remember. An attempt is made to find as to how far the customers are able to match the slogan with respective bank.

Table 2.5: Knowledge about Slogan (Punch Line)

Bank Brand(private sector)	Punch line	Total score	Mean Score	Rank
Axis	Everything is the same except the name	1346	2.32	2
CUB	Trust & excellence	1310	2.25	4
HDFC	We understand your world	1312	2.26	3
ICICI	Hum hai na	1359	2.34	1
Bank Brand(public sector)	**Punch line**	**Total score**	**Mean Score**	**Rank**
SBI	Pure banking nothing else	1350	2.32	1
BOB	India's international bank	1344	2.31	2

It is clear from the table that in the private sector, ICICI bank's punch line is most easily identified by customers followed by AXIS bank, HDFC bank and CUB.In the case of public sector, SBI bank punch line is most easily identified followed by BOB.

2.3.5. *Bank Preference*

Table 2.6: Important Reason behind Banking with Particular Bank

Reasons	Total Score	Mean Score	Ranks
Personal recommendation	17623	30.4	5
Price	22216	38.3	3
Well known Advertised	12823	22.1	6
Past experience	22657	39.1	2
Rating in consumer report	20414	35.2	4
Quality	26658	46.0	1

It is very obvious from the above table that the reason 'quality' is ranked first with the Garrett's score of 26658 points. It is followed by the reasons 'past experience' ranked second with the score of 22657points. The third rank is given for the reason 'price' with the score of 22216points. The reasons 'Rating in consumer report', 'Rating in consumer report' and'Well known Advertised' is ranked fourth, fifth and sixth with the scores of 20414, 17623 and 12823 points respectively.

2.4.   Summary

This chapter contains the origin and developments of Indian banking industry and the overall description of Commercial banks in India. The origin of banking in India, Structure of Indian banking system and the brief profile of the sample banks are discussed in this chapter.

Branding is building a trusting and lasting relationship with customer; and logos are visual symbols of brand recognition; if the logo, which represents the visual identity of the bank, is instantly recognizable by the customer, it signifies that the bank has build a brand."Effective logo must pass through the three stages of conceptualization, Commendation and commercialization. Conceptualization includes seven parameters of Theme, Look, Aesthetics, Complexity, Flexibility, Vulnerability and Memorability. Commendation stage involves appraisal and approval based degree of fit with the image of the bank. Commercialization includes launching the logo strategically and innovatively. Precisely, logos should reflect accurately the current identity of the organization, while at the same time be flexible for future development.

With regard to bank brands at the top of the mind among customers, SBI ranked first with the highest score of 2237 out of the selected sample banks. The second and third place goes to CUB and Indian bank with the score of 2156 and 2010 respectively.

It is evident that, in the case of private sector group, CUB ranked first with the highest score of 2156 and ICICI scored 1659 and got second position which clearly brings out the important place and brand power in the minds of customers. In the case of public sector group, SBI and Indian banks hold the first and second ranks.

In the public sector category SBI and Bank of Baroda stood first and second places with score of 1580 and 1573 respectively. In the private sector category, in terms logo identification ICICI bank ranked first with the highest score of 1520 and AXIS bank ranked second with the score of 1505.

It is found that 83.3% of customers got the knowledge about private sector banks through newspapers and in case of public sector banks 75% of the customers got knowledge about bank through bus painting.

It is clear that, in the private sector ICICI bank punch line is most easily identified by customers followed by AXIS bank, HDFC bank and CUB. In the case of public sector, SBI banks punch line is most easily identified followed by BOB.

It is found that important reason behind banking with the particular bank 'quality' is ranked first with the Garrett's score of 26658 points. It is followed by the reasons 'past experience' ranked second with the score of 22657 points. The third rank is given for the reason 'price' with the score of 22216 points. The reasons 'Rating in consumer report', 'Rating in consumer report' and 'Well known Advertised' is ranked fourth, fifth and sixth with the scores of 20414, 17623 and 12823 points respectively.

Chapter III

Customers' Perception on Brand Management in Commercial Banks

3.1. Introduction

Branding has become one of the most important aspects of business strategy. Branding plays an important role because positive brands will enable customers to better visualize and understand products, reduce customers' perceived risks in buying services, and help companies achieve sustained superior performance. In particular, brand image is a critical issue in the field of brand management. A good and effective brand normally has attributes which endure them to their loyal customers. According to Keller banks have understood the key to what makes them different: the relationship that develop between a customer and a banker under the support of the brand. A good brand name is critical in the financial services industry. It is important in the financial sector as it helps organize and label the myriad of new offerings in a manner that consumers can understand. Banks rely heavily on their reputation. After all, banking only works if the consumer is willing to trust the bank company with large sums of money.

Branding is particularly important to the financial sector in the current economy, since investors and other big spenders are being cautious about making large financial transactions. Structurally, bank brands are handicapped in that they cannot be illustrated. For banks today, the strength and marketing power of an institution's brand is rapidly becoming one of the critical level for differentiation and success. Banks need to provide a consistent brand experience to prevent customers from switching to rival banks. Hence, the field of bank service is now emphasizing the importance of customer-oriented marketing. Banks endeavor to establish marketing strategies which promote brand image among customers for enhancing the satisfaction and loyalty of customers as well as further promoting performance.

Now a day brand management has a growing importance in marketing, especially when companies try to transmit intangible and complex messages. How to prepare (provide) and develop a better understanding about the relationship between structures such as brand and customer loyalty is the main problem faced by brand managers. Marketing management literature has proposed many factors influencing customer loyalty. Perhaps the most important skill of a professional marketer is being able to create a strong brand, protect it, and strengthen it. Today, the aim of marketing is to manage demands through growth and move of customers to maturity up the loyalty ladder.

A brand name is an important guide for a potential customer. Like money, a brand name can facilitate transactions (bargains). Customers will be confused when they confront (face) mute products or products that do not have anything readable or products whose function (performance) cannot be assessed at a glance. Brand names and product prices make it easier for customers to understand the products. They can also eliminate uncertainty. A brand name is a summary of identity, originality, features and differences. A brand name puts and shows all these information in a word or a sign. For this reason, brand names are vital for business and transactions.

Environmental influences and marketing efforts can potentially lead to customer behavior changes. Customer loyalty to trademarks and brand names are also results of appropriate and strategic marketing activities. Loyalty is a complex concept. Loyalty as: A deep commitment to repurchase at future or commitment of additional purchase of a preferred product or service, whereby a repeated or similar brand will be purchased, despite environmental influences and marketing efforts which cause potential for behavioral changes.

Branding is critical in the banking industry given its integral role in society. In a time where there is increasing difficulty differentiating between banking industry, branding has never been more important. Branding gives a company a unique personality that sets it out from the rest and helps build the company a strong reputation and as well as creating value.

Strong brand stand for:

1. Branding is a key component in gaining **recognition**. Every aspect, from a website, to photography, to corporate design is defined by brand. Every touch point is an opportunity to increase brand perception and improve customer loyalty.
2. Branding creates and builds **trust**. Building a strong brand with loyal customer is of crucial importance as it provides considerable competitive and economic benefits to a banking industry. People are a lot more likely to do business with a company that is well polished and presented.
3. Branding is a valuable asset. Branding builds **financial value** and generates future business. Brands strengthen differentiation against peers, driving demand and sales, helping market share growth and building shareholder value.
4. A strong brand generates referral **business**, bringing new customer. People love telling others about brands they have positive experiences with.
5. Strong brands attract talent and **motivate staff**, giving them something to believe in and to stand behind.

Branding is at the heart of every business. It's vital to define what brand stands for. Brand is the way to perceive potential customer. It is fundamental to be aware of brand experience and to make sure it is an experience would want to have. Good branding elevates and differentiates products and services, and gives customer a reason to choose over peers. A strong brand doesn't just happen; it takes time, effort and a well thought out plan.

3.2. Quantification of Data and Measurement of Perception Level of the Customers

To measure the perception level of the customers, originally 49 statement have been used in the pilot study. On the basis of outcome of the pilot study and by using item analysis technique, two factors have been dropped. These statements were formed relating to Brand name, Service gap, Core service, Employee service, Self image congruence, Feeling, Controlled communication and uncontrolled communications. There components were contributed to perception score about the bank branding.

The sample customers are asked to respond to each statement relating to the customer perception towards brand management in commercial banks, using Rensis Likert's 5 point rating scale ranging from 'strongly agree' to 'strongly disagree'. If a customer is strongly agree with the statement, a scale value of 5 is assigned, scale value of 4 is assigned , if the response is well agree, 3 if the customer is neutral to some extent, 2 if the customer is disagree and 1 if the customer is strongly disagree. The total score for each sample customer from all 47 statements are calculated by using the above scoring procedure.

An individual's score is mere summation of scores secured from 47 statements of each sample customer. The scores of the sample customers range from 47 to 235. The average score is 141. Based on the average score, the sample customers have been grouped into two categories viz., Low Level (whose score is less than 141) and High Level (whose score is between 142 and 235).Classification of sample customers on the basis of their perception score are shown in Table 3.1.

Table 3.1: Classification of Sample Customers by Perception Score

Perception Level	Number of Customers	Per cent	Mean Score	S. D
Private sector banks				
Low Level	238	41.0	120.27	13.38
High Level	146	25.2	151.80	15.76
Total	384	66.2	132.26	20.97
Public sector banks				
Low Level	145	25.0	120.37	14.32
High Level	51	8.8	154.92	16.56
Total	196	33.8	129.36	21.27

Figures in parentheses are percentage

Table 3.1 shows that in the private sector banks majority (41.0%) of the sample customers are having low level perception about their banks and brand management. The mean score is 132.26 and standard deviation is 20.97. In the case of public sector banks (25.0%) of the sample customers are having low level perception about their banks and brand management. The mean score is 129.36 and standard deviation is 21.27.

3.3. Association between the Independent Variables of the Sample Customers and their Perception Level

It is expected that the independent variables of the sample customers would influence the perception level of the customers about their brand management in commercial banks. To examine the association between the perception level and independent variables, the following null hypothesis has been framed.

H_0: There is no significant association between the independent variables (age, gender, educational qualification, marital status, occupation, Annual income and annual balance) of the sample customers and their customer perception towards brand management in commercial banks.

This hypothesis has been tested with Chi-square test, 'F' test, 'Z' test and Contingency Co-efficient(C) at 1% level of significance.

3.3.1. Age and Perception Level

Age is the major factor in determining the perception level of customers. In the present study, an attempt has been made to examine the association between the age and perception level of the sample respondents. The respondents were classified as follows: Group A: 18 - 30 years; Group B: 31-50 years; and Group C: Above 50 years.

To test the hypothesis which states that the customers' perception level under different age groups does not differ significantly, Chi-square test was applied.

Table 3.2: Age and Perception Level: χ^2Test

Private Sector	Level of Perception		Total
Age Group	Low Level	High Level	
18 - 30 years	58(59.8)	39(40.2)	97(100)
31-50 years	150(61.0)	96(39.0)	246(100)
Above 50 years	30(73.2)	11(26.8)	41(100)
Total	238(62.0)	146(38.0)	384(100)
Ch-square value =2.289			

Public Sector	Level of Perception		Total
Age Group	Low Level	High Level	
18 - 30 years	61(81.3)	14(18.7)	75(100)
31-50 years	57(65.5)	30(34.5)	87(100)
Above 50 years	27(79.4)	7(20.6)	34(100)
Total	145(74.0)	51(26.0)	196(100)
Chi-square value =5.865			

Figures in parentheses are percentage

It is evident from the table 3.2 that in private sector banks respondents who are at the age of above 50 years low level perception compared to other age groups. From the above table it is found the public sector banks, higher percentage of respondents who are at the age of 31- 50 years have low level perception compared to other age groups.

In the case of Private sector (2.289) and Public sector (5.865) banks, the calculated values of chi-square are less than the table value (9.210)at 1% level of significance. Hence, the hypothesis is accepted. Therefore, it is inferred that there is no significant association between the age of the respondents and level of perception.

Average Perception Score of Customers on the Basis of Age

The average perception score of the three groups of respondents classified based on their age is given in the table 3.3.

Table 3.3: Age and Perception Score

Private Sector	Number of Customers	Total Score	Average Score
Age Group			
18 - 30 years	97(16.7)	12921	133.20
31-50 years	246(42.4)	32452	131.91
Above 50 years	41(7.1)	5416	132.09
Total	384(66.2)	50789	132.26
Public Sector	Number of Customers	Total Score	Average Score
Age Group			
18 - 30 years	75(12.9)	9545	127.26
31-50 years	87(15.0)	11411	131.16
Above 50 years	34(5.9)	4399	129.38
Total	196(33.8)	25355	129.36

Figures in parentheses are percentage

The table 3.3 point out that the average score of the respondents belonging to Group A sample customers is higher than that of other age groups in private sector banks (133.20). With regard to public sector bank, the average score of the respondents belonging to Group B (131.16) is higher than that of other age groups. To test the hypothesis that average score of the three groups of respondents classified on their age is the same, 'F' test was applied. The results are presented in Table 3.4.

Table 3.4: Age and Perception Level: 'F' Test

Source of Variation	Sum of Square	Df	Mean Square	'F' Value	Result
Between Samples	153.259	2	76.630	0.172	Insignificant
Within Samples	257748.368	577	446.704		
Total	257901.628	579			

It is evident from the Table 3.4that the calculated value (0.172) of 'F' is less than the Theoretical value (4.60). Hence, the framed null hypothesis is accepted and it can be concluded that there is a nosignificant difference in the mean score of the sample customers belonging to different age groups.

3.3.2. *Gender and Perception Level*

There is a general belief that gender of the customers would create an impact in their perception level. Hence, in the present study, an attempt has been made to identify the role played by gender of the sample customers in the aspect of perception level. The findings regarding the gender and perception level of the sample customers are shown in Table 3.5.

Table 3.5: Gender and Perception Level: χ^2Test

Private Sector	Level of Perception		Total
Gender	Low Level	High Level	
Male	148(65.2)	79(34.8)	227(100)
Female	90(57.3)	67(42.7)	157(100)
Total	238(62.0)	146(38.0)	384(100)
Chi-square value =2.441			
Public Sector	Level of Perception		Total
Gender	Low Level	High Level	
Male	86(74.5)	31(26.5)	117(100)
Female	59(73.7)	20(25.3)	79(100)
Total	145(74.0)	51(26.0)	196(100)
Chi-square value =0.034			

Figures in parentheses are percentage

Table 3.5 indicates that in private and public sector banks male customers are more than the female customers.

In the case of Private sector (2.441) and Public sector (0.034) banks, the calculated values of chi-square are less than the table value (6.635) at 1 % level of significance. Therefore, it is inferred that there is no significant association between the gender of the respondents and level of perception.

Average Perception Score of Customers on the Basis of Gender

The average perception score of the two groups of sample customers based on their gender is given in the table 3.6.

Table 3.6: Gender and Perception Score

Private Sector Gender	Number of Customers	Total Score	Average Score
Male	27(39.1)	29820	131.36
Female	157(27.1)	20969	133.56
Total	384(66.2)	50789	132.26
Public Sector Gender	**Number of Customers**	**Total Score**	**Average Score**
Male	117(20.2)	15245	127.97
Female	79(13.6)	10110	130.29
Total	196(33.8)	25355.00	129.36

Figures in parentheses are percentage

The table 3.6 indicates that in both private and public sector banks the average score of the sample respondents are more than the average score of the female respondents. To analyze the significance of the difference in the average score of the sample customers based on their gender, 'Z' test has been applied. Details of the findings are presented in Table 3.7.

Table 3.7: Gender and Perception Level: 'Z' Test

	Mean I $\overline{X_1}$	Mean II $\overline{X_2}$	MD $|\overline{X_1}-\overline{X_2}|$	SD	'Z' Value	Result
Private sector	1	2	3	4	5(3÷4)	Significant
	131.36	133.56	-2.2	-0.385	5.714	
Public sector	Mean I $\overline{X_1}$	Mean II $\overline{X_2}$	MD $|\overline{X_1}-\overline{X_2}|$	SD	'Z' Value	Result
	1	2	3	4	5(3÷4)	Significant
	127.97	130.29	-2.32	-0.383	6.057	

Table 3.7 shows that the calculated 'Z' value of private (5.714) and public sector banks (6.057) is exceeds the Table value (1.96). Hence, it can be concluded that there is significant difference in the average scores of the two categories based on the gender of the sample customers.

3.3.3. Marital Status and Perception Level

A person's Perception level may vary according to marital status. Hence, in order to test the association between the marital status and perception level, the sample customers are grouped into 2 categories viz., Married and Unmarried. The findings are shown in Table 3.8.

Table 3.8: Marital Status and Perception Level: χ²Test

Private Sector	Level of Perception		Total
Marital status	Low Level	High Level	
Married	177(63.0)	104(37.0)	281(100)
Unmarried	61(59.2)	42(40.8)	103(100)
Total	238(62.0)	146(38.0)	384(100)
Chi-square value =0.454			
Public Sector	Level of Perception		Total
Marital status	Low Level	High Level	
Married	87(69.0)	39(31.0)	126(100)
Unmarried	58(82.9)	12(17.1)	70(100)
Total	145(74.0)	51(26.0)	196(100)
Chi-square value =4.458			

Figures in parentheses are percentage

It is evident from the Table 3.8, in the case of private sector sample customers found that 63.0% of the married sample customers and 59.2% of the unmarried sample customers. In the case of public sector banks found that 82.9% of the unmarried and 69.0% married sample customers and are having low level perception about their banks.

In the case of private sector (0.454) and public sector (4.458) banks, the calculated value of Chi-square is less than the Table value(6.635). The framed null hypothesis is accepted. Therefore, it can be concluded that there is no significant association between the marital status and perception level of the sample customers.

Average Perception Scores of Customers on the Basis of Marital Status

The average perception score of the two groups of sample customers based on their marital status is given in the table 3.9.

Table 3.9: Marital Status and Perception Score

Private Sector Marital status	Number of Customers	Total Score	Average Score
Married	(281)48.4	37131	132.13
Unmarried	(103)17.8	13658	132.60
Total	(384)66.2	50789	132.26
Public Sector Marital status	Number of Customers	Total Score	Average Score
Married	(126)21.7	16414	130.26
Unmarried	(70)12.1	8941	127.72
Total	(196)33.8	25355	129.36

Figures in parentheses are percentage

From the Table 3.9, it is clear that in private sector banks unmarried sample customers' average score is greater than the married sample customers. In the case of the public sector banks married sample customers' average score is high compared to unmarried sample customers. It is proposed to test the significance of the difference in the average score of the sample customers based on marital status. For the purpose, 'Z' test is applied which is shown in Table 3.10.

Table 3.10: Marital Status and Perception Level: 'Z' Test

Private sector	Mean I $\overline{X_1}$	Mean II $\overline{X_2}$	MD $|\overline{X_1} - \overline{X_2}|$	SD	'Z' Value	Result
	1	2	3	4	5(3÷4)	Insignificant
	132.13	132.60	-0.47	0.485	0.969	
Public sector	Mean I $\overline{X_1}$	Mean II $\overline{X_2}$	MD $|\overline{X_1} - \overline{X_2}|$	SD	'Z' Value	Result
	1	2	3	4	5(3÷4)	Insignificant
	130.26	127.72	2.54	0.485	5.237	

Table 3.10 shows that the calculated 'Z' value of private sector (0.969) is less than table value and public sector banks (5.237) is exceeds the Table value. Hence, the framed null hypothesis is accepted. Thus, it can be concluded that there is no significant difference in the mean scores of the two categories based on the marital status of the sample customers.

3.3.4. *Educational Level and Perception Level*

Education enhances the knowledge of the customers about the services available for them. In the present study, the sample customers are from different educational background. Hence, an attempt has been made to examine the association between the educational level of the sample customers and their perception level. For the purpose of analysis, the sample customers are grouped into 4 categories viz., No Formal Education, School Level, UG Level and PG& above. The details of the findings are highlighted in Table 3.11.

Table 3.11: Educational Qualification and Perception Level: χ^2Test

Private Sector	Level of Perception		Total
Educational qualification	**Low Level**	**High Level**	
No Formal Education	24(60.0)	16(40.0)	40(100)
School Level	74(62.2)	45(37.8)	119(100)
UG Level	90(61.6)	56(38.4)	146(100)
PG &Above	50(63.3)	29(36.7)	79(100)
Total	238(62.0)	146(38.0)	384(100)
Chi-square value = 0.133			

Public Sector	Level of Perception		Total
Educational qualification	Low Level	High Level	
No Formal Education	11(52.4)	10(47.6)	21(100)
School Level	52(78.8)	14(21.2)	66(100)
UG Level	54(73.0)	20(27.0)	74(100)
PG &Above	28(80.0)	7(20.0)	35(100)
Total	145(74.0)	51(26.0)	196(100)
Chi-square value =6.580			

Figures in parentheses are percentage

Table 3.11 shows that, in the case of private sector 63.3% of the PG & Above, 62.2% of the School Level, 61.6% of the UG Level and 60.0% of the No Formal Education sample customers are having low level perception. In the case of public sector 80.0% of the PG & Above, 78.8% of the School level, 73.0 % of the UG Level and 52.4% No Formal Education sample customers are having low perception.

In the case of private sector (0.133) and public sector (6.580) banks, the calculated value of Chi-square is less than the Table value (11.345). The framed null hypothesis is accepted. Therefore, it can be concluded that there is no significant association between the Educational qualification and perception level of the sample customers.

Average Perception Scores of Customers on the Basis of Educational Qualification

The average perception score of the four groups of sample customers based on their educational qualification is given in the table 3.12.

Table 3.12: Educational Qualification and Perception Score

Private Sector Educational qualification	Number of Customers	Total Score	Average Score
No Formal Education	40(6.9)	5346	133.65
School Level	119(20.5)	15456	129.88
UG Level	146(25.2)	19326	132.36
PG &Above	79(13.6)	10661	134.94
Total	384(66.2)	50789	132.26
Public Sector Educational qualification	Number of Customers	Total Score	Average Score
No Formal Education	21(3.6)	2897	137.95
School Level	66(11.4)	8335	126.28
UG Level	74(12.8)	9663	130.58
PG &Above	35(6.0)	4460	127.42
Total	196(33.8)	25355	129.36

Figures in parentheses are percentage

From the Table 3.12, it is clear that in both public and private sector banks the No formal education average score is high compared to others. It is proposed to test the significance of the difference in the average score of the sample customers based on Educational qualification. For the purpose, 'F' test is applied which is shown in Table 3.13.

Table 3.13: Educational Qualification and Perception Level: 'F' Test

Source of Variation	Sum of Square	Df	Mean Square	'F' Value	Result
Between Samples	2496.845	3	832.282	1.877	Insignificant
Within Samples	255404.782	576	443.411		
Total	257901.628	579			

Table 3.13 highlights that the calculated value of (1.877)of 'F' is less than the Theoretical value of 3.78. Hence, the framed null hypothesis is accepted and it can be concluded that the no association between the mean score of the sample customers with different level of education and perception level is found to be significant.

3.3.5. Occupational Status and Perception Level

The perception level of the people may vary according to their occupational status. An attempt is made to examine the association between the occupational status and perception level of the sample customers. For this purpose, the sample customers are grouped into5 categories viz., Business, Employed, Agricultural, Student/Housewife and pensioner. The distribution of the sample customers according to their occupational status and perception level is shown in Table 3.14.

Table 3.14: Occupational Status and Perception Level: χ^2Test

Private Sector	Level of Perception		Total
Occupational status	Low Level	High Level	
Business	38(57.6)	28(42.4)	66(100)
Employed	79(59.8)	53(40.2)	132(100)
Agricultural	73(66.4)	37(33.6)	110(100)
Student/Housewife	44(63.8)	25(36.2)	69(100)
pensioner	4(57.1)	3(42.9)	7(100)
Total	238(62.0)	146(38.0)	384(100)
Chi-square value = 1.854			
Private Sector	Level of Perception		Total
Occupational status	Low Level	High Level	
Business	47(82.5)	10(17.5)	57(100)
Employed	35(70.0)	15(30.0)	50(100)
Agricultural	46(74.2)	16(25.8)	62(100)
Student/Housewife	8(57.1)	6(42.9)	14(100)
pensioner	9(69.2)	4(30.8)	13(100)
Total	145(74.0)	51(26.0)	196(100)
Chi-square value =4.754			

Figures in parentheses are percentage

Table 3.14 shows that, in the case of private sector 66.4% of the Agricultural, 63.8% of the Student/Housewife, 59.8% Employed,57.6% of the Business and 57.1 pensioner sample customers are having low level perception. In the case of public sector 82.5% of the Business, 74.2% of the Agricultural, 70.0% Employed, 69.2% of the pensioner and 57.1 Student/Housewife sample customers are having low level perception.

In the case of private sector (1.858) and public sector (4.754) banks, the calculated value of Chi-square is less than the Table value (13.277). The framed null hypothesis is accepted. Therefore, it can be concluded that there is no significant association between the Occupational status and perception level of the sample customers.

Average Perception Scores of Customers on the Basis of Occupational Status

The average perception score of the five groups of sample customers based on their occupational status is given in the table 3.15.

Table 3.15: Occupational Status and Perception Score

Private Sector Occupational status	Number of Customers	Total Score	Average Score
Business	66(11.4)	8783	133.07
Employed	132(22.8)	17699	134.08
Agricultural	110(19.0)	14412	131.01
Student/Housewife	69(11.9)	8931	129.43
Pensioner	7(1.2)	964	137.71
Total	384(66.2)	50789	132.26
Public Sector Occupational status	**Number of Customers**	**Total Score**	**Average Score**
Business	57(9.8)	7405	129.91
Employed	50(8.6)	6336	126.72
Agricultural	62(10.7)	8033	129.56
Student/Housewife	14(2.4)	1877	134.07
Pensioner	13(2.2)	1704	131.07
Total	196(33.8)	25355	129.36

Figures in parentheses are percentage

From the Table 3.15, it is clear that the average score of the respondents in pensioner sample customers is greater that of other groups in private sector banks. With regard to public sector banks, the average score of the respondents in Student/Housewife (134.07) is higher than the other groups. It is proposed to test the significance of the difference in the average score of the sample customers based on Occupational Status. For the purpose, 'F' test is applied which is shown in Table 3.16.

Table 3.16: Occupational Status and Perception Level: 'F' Test

Source of Variation	Sum of Square	Df	Mean Square	'F' Value	Result
Between Samples	414.134	4	103.533	0.231	Insignificant
Within Samples	257487.494	575	447.804		
Total	257901.628	579			

Table 3.16 shows that the calculated value (0.231) of 'F' is less than the Theoretical value(3.78). Thus, it can be concluded that the no association between the mean score of the sample customers and perception level is found to be insignificant.

3.3.6. *Annual Income and Perception Level*

Income will influence the life style of the people. Income of the sample customers may also determine their perception level. Hence, the annual income is another essential one to assess the perception level. The perception level of the customers in different annual income group may vary. Based on their annual family income, the sample customers are classified into three groups viz., A (Upto Rs.2,00,000), B (Rs.2,00,001 to Rs.5,00,000) and C (Above Rs.5,00,000). The details of the findings are shown in the Table 3.17.

Table 3.17: Annual Income and Perception Level: χ^2Test

Private Sector	Level of Perception		Total
Annual income	Low Level	High Level	
Up toRs. 2,00,000	119(61.7)	74(38.3)	193(100)
Rs. 2,00,001 to Rs.5,00,000	96(63.2)	56(36.8)	152(100)
Above Rs.5,00,000	23(59.0)	16(41.0)	39(100)
Total	238(62.0)	146(38.0)	384(100)
Chi-square value = 0.247			
Public Sector	**Level of Perception**		**Total**
Annual income	Low Level	High Level	
Up to Rs.2,00,000	67(72.0)	26(28.0)	93(10)
Rs. 2,00,001 to Rs. 5,00,000	60(74.1)	21(25.9)	81(100)
Above Rs. 5,00,000	18(81.8)	4(18.2)	22(100)
Total	145(74.0)	51(26.0)	196(100)
Chi-square value =0.884			

Figures in parentheses are percentage

Table 3.17 shows clearly reveals that with regard to public and private sector banks Group B sample customers are low level of perception.

In the case of private sector (0.247) and public sector (0.884) banks, the calculated value of Chi-square is less than the Table value (9.210). The framed null hypothesis is accepted. Therefore, it can be concluded that there is no significant association between the Annual income and perception level of the sample customers.

Average Perception Scores of Customers on the Basis of Annual Income

The average perception score of the three groups of sample customers based on their annual income is given in the following table.

Table 3.18: Annual Income and Perception Score

Private Sector Annual income	Number of Customers	Total Score	Average Score
Up to Rs. 2,00,000	193(33.3)	25431	131.76
Rs. 2,00,001 to Rs. 5,00,000	152(26.2)	20178	132.75
Above Rs. 5,00,000	39(6.7)	5180	132.82
Total	384(66.2)	50789	132.26
Public Sector Annual income	Number of Customers	Total Score	Average Score
Up to Rs. 2,00,000	93(16.0)	12168	130.83
Rs. 2,00,001 to Rs. 5,00,000	81(14.0)	10408	128.49
Above Rs. 5,00,000	22(3.8)	2779	126.31
Total	196(33.8)	25355	129.36

Figures in parentheses are percentage

From the Table 3.18, it is found that the average score of the sample respondents who are in high income group is higher than (132.82) that of other groups in private sector banks. With regards to public sector banks, the average score of the customers in low income (130.83) is higher than that of other groups. In order to test the significance between the mean score of the sample customers on the basis of their annual income and perception level, 'F' test has been applied which is shown in Table 3.19.

Table 3.19: Annual Income and Perception Level: 'F' Test

Source of Variation	Sum of Square	Df	Mean Square	'F' Value	Result
Between Samples	49.298	2	24.649	0.055	Insignificant
Within Samples	257852.329	577	446.884		
Total	257901.628	579			

It is evident from the Table 3.19 that the calculated value (0.055) of 'F' is less than the Theoretical value (4.60). Therefore, it can be concluded that the no association between the mean score of the sample customers on the basis of their annual income and perception level of the sample customers is found to be insignificant.

3.3.7. *Annual Balance and Perception Level*

The people save the money for future period of time. One of the main objectives of the banks is to mobilize savings among the people. There may be some relationship between the saving habit of the customers and their perception level. An attempt has been made to analyze the association between the annual savings and the perception level of the sample customers.

For the analysis purpose, the sample customers are grouped into four groups viz., Less than 1Lakh, 1 Lakh to 3Lakhs, 3Lakhs to 5Lakhsand Above 5Lakhs. The findings are shown in Table 3.20.

Table 3.20: Annual Balance and Perception Level: χ^2Test

Private Sector	Level of Perception		Total
Annual Balance	**Low Level**	**High Level**	
Less than 1Lakh	46(56.1)	36(43.9)	82(100)
1 Lakh to 3Lakhs	87(68.5)	40(31.5)	127(100)
3Lakhs to 5lakhs	70(61.9)	43(38.1)	113(100)
Above 5lakhs	35(56.5)	7(43.5)	62(100)
Total	238(62.0)	146(38.0)	384(100)
Chi-sq uare value = 4.302			

Public Sector	Level of Perception		Total
Annual Balance	**Low Level**	**High Level**	
Less than 1Lakh	23(74.2)	8(25.8)	31(100)
1Lakh to 3Lakhs	29(64.4)	16(35.6)	45(100)
3Lakhs to 5lakhs	61(77.2)	18(22.8)	79(100)
Above 5lakhs	32(78.04)	9(22.0)	41(100)
Total	145(74.0)	51(26.0)	196(100)
Chi-square value =3.097			

Figures in parentheses are percentage

The table 3.20 shows, that with regard to private sector banks, 68.5% are sample customer maintain annual Income of Rs.1Lakh to Rs.3Lakhs and public sector banks, 70.04% of the above 5Lakhs respondents have low perception than the respondents of other groups

In the case of private sector (4.302) and public sector (3.097) banks, the calculated value of Chi-square is less than the Table value (11.345). The framed null hypothesis is accepted. Therefore, it can be concluded that there is no significant association between the Annual balance and perception level of the sample customers.

Average Perception Scores of Customers on the Basis of Annual Balance

The average perception score of the three groups of sample customers based on their annual balance is given in the following table.

Table 3.21: Annual Balance and Perception Score

Private Sector Annual Balance	Number of Customers	Total Score	Average Score
Less than 1Lakh	82(14.1)	11098	135.34
1Lakh to 3Lakhs	127(21.9)	16601	130.71
3Lakhs to 5lakhs	113(19.5)	14809	131.05
Above 5lakh	62(10.7)	8281	133.56
Total	384(66.2)	50789	132.26
Public Sector Annual Balance	**Number of Customers**	**Total Score**	**Average Score**
Less than 1Lakh	31(5.3)	3877	125.06
1 Lakh to 3Lakhs	45(7.8)	5914	131.42
3Lakhs to 5lakhs	79(13.6)	10242	129.64
Above 5lakh	41(7.0)	5322	129.76
Total	196(33.8)	25355	129.36

Figures in parentheses are percentage

From the Table 3.21, it is found that the average score of the sample respondents who are in less than the 1 lakh group is higher than (135.34) that of other groups in private sector banks. With regards to public sector banks, the average score of the customers in 1 lakh to 3 lakhs (131.42) is higher than that of other groups. To test the significance in the difference between the mean score of the sample customers on the basis of their annual balance and perception level, 'F' test has been applied. Details of the findings are shown in Table 3. 22.

Table 3.22: Annual Balance and Perception Level: 'f' test

Source of Variation	Sum of Square	Df	Mean Square	'F' Value	Result
Between Samples	390.190	4	97.547	0.218	Insignificant.
Within Samples	257511.438	575	447.846		
Total	257901.628	579			

It is evident from the Table 3.22 that the calculated value (0.218) of 'F' is less than the Theoretical value (3.32). Therefore, it can be concluded that the no association between the mean score of the sample customers on the basis of their annual balance and perception level of the sample customers is found to be insignificant.

3.4. Perception Level of the Customer Regarding Brand Management in Commercial Banks: Multiple Regression Analysis

This section is devoted to a discussion on the variables influencing the perception of the customers. In this connection, the hypothesis that the perception of the customers is influenced by age, gender, marital status, educational qualification, occupation, annual income, total experience with this banks is tested with the help of Regression Analysis. The test aims at finding out whether the independent variables (X1, X_2, X_3.....X_7) do actually have any significant influence on the dependent variable (Y).

Regression analysis is used to make prediction about the level and type of association exists between two variables. Simple or Bivariate regression analysis is a statistical technique that uses information about the relationship between one independent variable and a dependent variable.

Multiple regression analysis is the most appropriate technique to examine the combined influence of several independent variables on one dependent variable of interest. Multiple independent variables were entered into the same regression equation, and for each variable, a separate regression coefficient is calculated that describes its relationship with the dependent variable. These coefficients examine the relative influence of each independent variable and dependent variable. The type of relationship that exists between each independent variable and dependent measure is still linear. However, with the addition of multiple independent variables, one should think of multiple independent dimensions instead of just a straight-line description.

Regression analysis involves estimating an equation, which is usually a linear one and independent variables are considered to be statistically independent. It is well known that multi-collinearity does not exist in case of large samples[1].

The Multiple Linear Equation is:

$$Y = b_0 + b_1 X_1 + b_2 X_2 + b_3 X_3 + b_4 X_4 + b_5 X_5 + b_6 X_6 + b_7 X_7$$

Where Y=Total Perception score on Brand Management in Commercial Banks

X_1=Age

X_2=Gender

X_3=Educational qualification

X_4=Marital status

X_5=Occupation

X_6=Annual income

X_7=Total experience with the bank

b_0=Regression constant, and

b_1, b_2, b_3....b_7=Regression coefficients of independent variables

---

[1] Srivastava, V. K., Shenoy, G. V. and Sharma, S. C. *1997. Quantitative Techniques for Managerial Decisions*, New Delhi: New Age International, p. 345.

The easiest way to analyze the relationships is to examine the regression coefficients for each independent variable. These coefficients still describe the average amount of change to be expected in Y given a unit change in the value of the particular independent variable. Moreover, each particular regression coefficient describes the strength of the relationship between an individual independent variables and the dependent variable.

With the addition of more than one independent variable, a couple of new issues have to be considered. One concern is the possibility that each independent variable may be measured using a different scale. When multiple independent variables are measured with different scales, it is not possible to make relative comparisons between regression coefficients to see which independent variable has the most influence on the dependent variable.

To solve this problem, standardized regression coefficient is to be calculated. It is called **Beta Coefficient,** and it is calculated from the Normal Regression Coefficient. The regression coefficient is recalculated to have a mean of zero and a standard deviation of one. Standardization removes the effects of using different scales of measurement. Beta coefficients will range from 0.00 to 1.00. Use of the beta coefficient allows direct comparisons between independent variables to determine which variables have the most influence on the dependent measure.[2]

After the regression coefficients are estimated, the statistical significance of each coefficient should be examined. This is done in the same manner as the bivariate regression. Each regression coefficient will be divided by its standard error to produce a student's 't' statistic, which was compared against the critical value to determine whether the null hypothesis can be rejected. Many times not all the independent variables in a regression equation will be statistically significant. Practically, if a regression coefficient is not statistically significant, that means the independent variable does not have a relationship with the dependent variable and the slope describing that relationship is relatively flat. That is, the value of the dependent variable does not change at all as the value of the statistically insignificant independent variable changes.

The results of a regression model are tested to examine its significance include the R^2; the model F statistic; the individual regression coefficients for each independent variable; their associate 't' statistics; and the individual beta coefficients. The appropriate procedure to follow in evaluating the results of a regression analysis is as follows:

---

[2] Joseph F.Hair, Robert P.Bush and David J.Ortinau, *Marketing Research*, New Delhi: Tata McGraw Hill Publishing Company Limited, 2003, P.578.

- Assess the statistical significance of the overall regression model using the F statistic and its associated probability;
- Evaluate the obtained R^2 to see how large it is;
- Examine the individual regression coefficient to assess relative influence.

Coefficient of determination (R^2) describes the strength of the relationships between all the independent variables in the equation and the dependent variable. It is a measure of the amount of variation in the dependent variable associated with (explained by) the variation in the independent variable. Higher values for R^2 mean stronger relationship between the group of independent variables and the dependent measure.

'F' test was appropriate for conducting joint tests of significance. i.e. tests of the significance of all $b_0, b_1, b_2 \ldots b_7$ in the equation. The 'F' ratio for the regression model indicates the statistical significance of the overall regression model. The F ratio is the result of comparing the amount of explained variance to the unexplained variance. The larger the F ratio, the more variance on the dependent variable is associated with the independent variable.

Hence, regression analysis is used to examine the relationship between perception age score of the respondents and independent variables such as, gender, marital status, educational qualification, occupation, annual income, bank's branch, average annual balance, types of accounts maintained in this branch and total experience with this bank.

In this study, seven separate regression equation Models are worked out to ascertain the influence of different sets of independent variables on perception. The regressions are estimated using cross-section data of 580 respondents.

REGRESSION MODEL: $Y = f(X1, X_2, X_3, X_4, X_5 \text{ and } X_7)$

Regression equation is developed by increasing the number of independent variables to seven. Multiple regression analysis provides information to test the following hypothesis.

H_o : There is no relationship between satisfaction (Y) and independent variables X_1, $X_2, \ldots X_7$.

Table 3.22 shows the results of estimated regression equation of Y on $X_1, X_2, \ldots X_7$.

The regression equation for private sector is,

$$Y = 168.893 + 0.236X_1 + 1.371X_2 - 0.393X_3 + 3.628X_4 - 0.54X_5 - 0.458X_6 - 0.644X_7.$$

The regression equation for public sector is,

$$Y = 166.736 + 2.012X_1 - 3.69X_2 + 2.154X_3 - 0.678X_4 - 0.493X_5 + 0.764X_6 - 1.099X_7.$$

Table 3.23: Results of regression equation of Y on X_1, X_2, ... X_7

Variables	Private banks		Public banks	
	Unstandardised Coefficients	't' statistic	Unstandardised Coefficients	't' statistic
Constant	168.893	77.226	166.736	23.828
Age	0.236	1.237	2.012	2.646**
Gender (Male)	1.371	2.895**	-3.69	-3.036**
Educational qualification	0.393	3.036**	2.154	3.303**
Marital status (Married)	3.628	4.505**	-0.678	-0.567
Occupation	0.54	-1.991*	-0.493	-0.989
Annual income	-0.458	-0.877	0.764	0.906
Total experience with this bank	-0.644	-2.624**	-1.099	-2.167*
'R'	0.726		0.739	
'R²'	0.607		0.682	
$\overline{R}^2$	0.327		0.315	
'F'	26.447(0.000)		23.49(0.000)	

** - Significant at 1% level

*- Significant at 5% level

From the above table it is found that the 32.7% of variation in the perception level of private banks and 31.5% of variation in the perception level public banks are explained through the selected independent variables.

The age factor in the public sector group has influenced the perception level positively (β = 2.01; t = 2.64) at five percent level. This proved that increase age is the reason for positive perception level.

The Gender factor in the private sector group has influenced the perception positively (β = 1.371; t = 2.895) at five percent level. This proved that increase gender is the reason for positive perception level.

The gender factor in the public sector group has influenced the perception positively (β = -3.69; t = -3.036) at five percent level. This proved that increase gender is the reason for positive perception level.

The educational qualification factor in the private sector group has influenced the perception positively (β = 0.393; t = 3.036) at five percent level. This proved that increase educational qualification is the reason for positive perception level.

The educational qualification factor in the public sector group has influenced the perception positively (β = 2.154; t = 3.303) at five percent level. This proved that increase educational qualification is the reason for positive perception level.

The marital status factor in the private sector group has influenced the perception positively (β = 3.628; t = 4.505) at five percent level. This proved that marital status is the reason for positive perception level.

The occupation factor in the private sector group has influenced the perception positively (β = 0.54; t = 1.991) at one percent level. This proved that increase occupation is the reason for positive perception level.

The total experience with this bank factor in the private sector group has influenced the perception negatively (β = -0.644; t = -2.624) at five percent level. This proved that decrease total experience with this bank is the reason for negative perception level.

The total experience with this bank factor in the public sector group has influenced the perception positively (β = -1.099; t = -2.167) at one percent level. This proved that decrease total experience with this bank is the reason for negative perception level.

3.5. Summary

In this chapter, the perception level of the customers about their banks and brand management has been examined. In order to examine the perception level, required primary data have been collected by using questionnaire. For which, 21 relevant statements have been given in the questionnaire by using Rensis Likert's 5 point rating scale technique. Such collected data have been analysed with the help of various statistical tools like Standard Deviation, Chi-square, Contingency Co-efficient at 1% level of significance, 'F' test, 'Z' test and Multiple Regression Analysis.

It is found that majority of the sample customers in private sector banks are having low level perception about their banks and brand management. The mean score is 132.26 and standard deviation is 20.97. In the case of public sector banks majority (25.0%) of the sample customers are having low level perception about their banks and brand management. The mean score is 129.36 and standard deviation is 21.27.

In age-wise analysis, it is found that private sector banks respondents who are at the age of above 50 years low level perception compared to other age groups. In the case of public sector banks, higher percentage of respondents who are at the age of 31- 50 years have low level perception compared to other age groups.

In gender- wise analysis, it is found that private and public sector banks male customers are more than the female customers.

While considering the marital status, it is clear that the mean score private sector banks unmarried sample customers is greater than the married sample customers. In the case of the public sector banks married customers high compared to unmarried sample customers.

Regarding the educational level, in the case of private sector 63.3% of the PG & Above, 62.2% of the School level, 61.6% of the UG Level and 60.0% of the No formal education sample customers are having low level perception. In the case of public sector 80.0% of the PG & Above, 78.8% of the School level, 73.0 % of the UG Level and 52.4% No formal education sample customers are having low perception.

While examining the occupational status, in the case of private sector 66.4% of the Agricultural, 63.8% of the Student/Housewife, 59.8% Employed, 57.6% of the Business and 57.1 pensioner sample customers are having low level perception. In the case of public sector 82.5% of the Business, 74.2% of the Agricultural, 70.0% Employed, 69.2% of the pensioner and 57.1 Student/Housewife sample customers are having low level perception.

In the aspect of the annual income, both of private sector & public sector banks Rs 2,00,001 to 5,00,000 sample customers are having low level perception about brand management.

While considering the annual balance, found that with regard to private sector banks, 68.5% of the 1Lakh to 3Lakhs and public sector banks and 78.04% of the above 5Lakhs respondents' low perception than the respondents of other groups.

From the inferences of the results of Chi-square test, it is found that the socio-economic characteristics of the sample customers like age, gender, educational level, marital status, occupational status, annual income and annual balance have a no significant association with perception level of the sample customers about their brand management in commercial banks.

In 'F' test, it is found that the association between various socio-economic characteristics like age, gender, educational level, marital status, occupational status, annual income and annual balance of the sample customers and their perception level is found to be insignificant.

From the results of 'Z' test, it can be concluded that there is significant difference in the mean scores of gender and marital status (private sector banks) and there is a no significant difference in the mean scores of the marital status (public sector banks) and perception level of the sample customers about their brand management in commercial banks.

In Multiple Regression Analysis, it is found that the independent variables explain about 68.2% of the variation in the dependent variable.

CHAPTER IV

CUSTOMERS' ATTITUDE TOWARDS BRAND MANAGEMENT IN COMMERCIAL BANKS

4.1. Introduction

Measuring customer attitude has become a buzzword in the contemporary business world. In recent days consumer's attitude has become an important area for the commercial banks. The banking industry is a service industry and provides its customers with variety of financial services. Therefore a banking organization must prioritize the provision of high quality service to its customers. This will help to gain positive attitude from customers and also retaining the brand management in the present era. People are using the services of the banks to meet up their variety of purposes. Services delivered by the banks play an important role in forming customer's attitude towards the organizations. Banks are the financial service providers, producing and selling management of the public funds as well as performing various significant roles in the economy of any country. Globally banking process and its area are spreading faster as well as getting wider day by day. Recently, several private banks are operating their activities since long time. They are playing a vital role in enhancing the quality of the banking services in our country to achieve positive customer's attitude. This study involves a survey which has been conducted to discover customer attitudes towards brand management in commercial banks. This study will help to find out the attitudes of the customers on the services provided by the banks.

Building strong brand equity is not easy, it takes the commitment of the stakeholders, top management and the consistent implementation of marketing communications programmes. Further, it bridges the expectations of consumers and companies promise a product to its consumers. Products that have the brand power will meet the expectations of consumers and the consumer will make the decision. In maintaining brand equity, can be done through proper marketing communications.

Factors Affecting Customers' Attitude in Banking Industry

Banking industry is one of the industries where consumer's attitudes play an important role. People deposit their money into the banks and banks on the other hand lend it to different organizations. In a country there exists many financial organizations and different people choose different banks based on their attitudes and preferences. Some people may look for high interest rate and other may look for smooth services. Consumers' attitude towards the banking services depends on several factors. First of all the location of a bank can have different attitudes on people's mind. People may choose a bank which is very near to their home. Some people may choose their financial institutions based on its internal environment. The behavior of the employees plays an important attitude in developing customers' attitude. Here employees should be very much friendly giving much emphasis on customers' preference. Degree of complexity in terms of transactions is another important factor in developing customer's attitude. Some banks have introduced with modern technology which helps to develop positive customer's attitude. Some banks are providing unique services e.g. night banking, online banking which is also helpful to develop positive customers' attitude. Some customers prefer to be given individual care and attention from their financial institution and if they do not receive this, it may have a negative impact on the customers' attitude. Another important factor is customers always want to feel relax about the safety of their deposits. Deposits are the main asset of a bank. Therefore banks should keep customers informed that their deposits are safe which will help to develop a positive attitude to their banks. If a well reputed bank fails to meet customers' expectation, this might negatively affect the brand image of that bank. In addition to this there are some other factors e.g. reliability and credibility, services charge, Objection handling, hospitality (inviting decoration, waiting time hospitality), delivering services as promised, variety of products,internal environment, employees skill etc. which are responsible for developing positive or negative attitude of customer to the banking sectors. Therefore marketer should always be careful in delivering services so that customers can have a positive attitude toward their services.

Brand is a simple but very confused word with multiple meanings. Within this field, there are a number of generally accepted definitions. These variously refer to the brand as "a product or service, which a customer perceives to have distinctive benefits beyond price and functional performance" or "a symbol serving to distinguish the products and services of one company from another". A brand may have many other meanings depending on the role it plays, the value it has and more importantly, to whom it is related. To brand owners, a brand is mainly a differentiation device: the living memory and the future of its products. In the most developed role, brands represent not only the products or services a company provides but the firm itself, the brand is the company and brands become a synonym of the company's policy. In product-based marketing, the term brand is defined as "a distinguishing name and/or symbol intended to identify the goods or services of either seller or a group of sellers, and to differentiate those goods or services from those of competitors". Branding is a key function in marketing that means much more than just giving a product a name. The conventional wisdom of branding believes that the ultimate aim of branding is to command a favorable position in the mind of consumers, distinct from competition.

The objectives in branding can be summarized as follows:

- To dominate the market (to reduce or eliminate competition);
- To increase customer loyalty (by increasing the switch cost);
- To raise the entry barriers (to fend off potential threat).

Branding yields different advantages for firms. Organizations develop brands as a way to attract and keep customers by promoting value, image, prestige, or lifestyle. By using a particular brand, a consumer can cement a positive image. Brands can also reduce the risk, consumers face when buying something that they know little about. Once consumers become accustomed to a certain brand, they do not readily accept substitutes. A brand is also flexible, allowing firms to position and appeal to different segments in different markets. A successful brand is believed to bring its owner great financial value in terms of either higher sales or premium prices and give employees the satisfaction and confidence in their products or services. Strong branding can also accelerate market awareness and acceptance of new products entering the market. It seems that consumer's attitudes and opinions have an important role in branding research. In psychology, attitude is believed to be the major determinant of future decision-making. However, little is known about the relationship between branding and customers' attitudes. With strong branding, banks can attract customers and create customers' trust and loyalty to the bank. It also enhances the effectiveness of promotional campaigns of competitors, hence; brand equity is an asset to create a difference and increases the chances of success for the bank.

The success ofa brand depends on the level of value that customers perceived. Commercial banks have recently become more interested in building and developing their brands. Bank brand equity has increasingly become an important factor in a number of banking performances. This chapter mainly focused on the brand attitude on potential customers.

4.2. Quantification of Data and Measurement of Attitude Level of the Sample Respondents

To measure the attitude level of the customer Rensis Likert's summarised scaling techniques was adopted. 33 statements were prepared from a search of literature and academic experts. On the basis of outcome of the pilot study and by using item analysis technique one statement have been dropped. Finally, 32 statements are identified as significant and the same have been used in the final questionnaire for data collection. These statements were formed relating to Brand attitude, Brand verdict, Opinion about bank and future aspects.

Questionnaire was used as an instrument for collecting primary data, each statement relating to the attitude level about brand management in banking sector, using Rensis Likert's 5 point rating scale ranging from 'Strongly Agree' to 'Strongly Disagree'. If a respondent is strongly agree with the statement, a scale value of 5 is assigned, scale value of 4 is assigned , if the scheme is agree, 3 if the respondents are neutral to some extent, 2 if the respondents are disagree and 1 if the respondents are highly disagree. The total score for each sample respondents from all 32 statements are calculated using the above scoring procedure.

4.3. Association between the Demographic Variables of the Sample Respondents and their Attitude Level

It is expected that the demographic variables of the sample respondents would influence the attitude level of the respondents about banks. To examine the association between the attitude level and demographic variables, the following null hypothesis has been framed.

H_o: There is no significant association between the demographic variables (Age, Gender, Educational Qualification, Marital status, Occupation, Annual Income and Total Experience) of the sample respondents and their attitude level about the private sector banks.

This hypothesis has been tested with Chi-square test at 5% level of significance in two banks separately.

Table 4.1: Demographic Variables and Attitude Level: χ^2Test Private Sector

Demographic Variables	Pearson Chi-square Value	Df	Asymp. Sig. (2-sided)	Result
Age	21.456	8	0.024	Rejected
Gender	4.832	4	0.003	Rejected
Educational Qualification	8.507	12	0.744	Accepted
Marital status	26.172	4	0.000	Rejected
Occupation	14.599	16	0.034	Rejected
Annual Income	29.282	8	0.000	Rejected
Total Experience	13.866	20	0.567	Accepted

Source: Primary Data

Table 4.1 points out the results of Chi-square analysis of Private sector banks. The null hypothesis is rejected with regard to demographic variables viz., Age, Gender, Marital status, Occupation and Annual Income and p value is less than the significance level of 0.05 and it is concluded that there is an association between these five variables of the respondents and the attitude level towards brand management in banking sector. The values of Educational Qualification and Total Experience are more than p value at the significance level of 0.05 and it is noted the null hypothesis is accepted and there is no significant association between these two demographic variables and the attitude level towards brand management in banking sector.

Table 4.2: Demographic Variables and Attitude Level: χ^2 Test Pubic Sector

Demographic Variables	Pearson Chi-square Value	df	Asymp. Sig. (2-sided)	Result
Age	31.229	8	0.000	Rejected
Gender	4.210	4	0.013	Rejected
Educational Qualification	16.664	12	0.027	Rejected
Marital status	16.521	4	0.034	Rejected
Occupation	16.236	16	0.004	Accepted
Annual Income	17.562	8	0.045	Rejected
Total Experience	10.349	20	0.961	Accepted

Source: Primary Data

Table 4.2 points out the results of Chi-square analysis of public sector. The null hypothesis is rejected with regard to demographic variables viz., Age, Gender, Educational Qualification, Marital status and Annual Income and p value is less than the significance level of 0.05 and it is concluded that there is an association between these five demographic variables of the respondents and the attitude level towards brand management in banking sector. With regard to Occupation and Total Experience are more than p value at the significant level of 0.05 and it is noted the null hypothesis is accepted and there is no significant association between these two variables and the attitude level towards brand management in banking sector.

4.4. Attitude Level of the Respondents about Brand Management: Reliability Test-Cronbach's Alpha

The required primary data collected from the sample respondents in order to measure the attitude level of the respondents about brand management is collected through 5 point Likert's scale technique using 32 relevant statements. The validity of the statements is measured through Reliability analysis. Cronbach's Alpha is the most common measure of internal consistency[1]. In the present study, reliability analysis is applied to measure the reliability and internal consistency of the variables used to measure the attitude level. The reliability statistics provides the actual value for Cronbach's Alpha. It is shown in Table 4.3

---

[1] https://stastistics.laerd.com/cronbachs-alpha-using-spss.statistics.php, retrieved on 12.05.2015.

Table 4.3: Reliability Statistics: Cronbach's Alpha

Cronbach's Alpha	Number of Items
0.878	32

It is clear from the Table 4.3that the calculated value of Cronbach's Alpha is 0.878 for 32 items used for the analysis. The value is below the suitable range (ie., between 0.90 and 1.00). Therefore, it can be concluded that the factors used to measure the attitude level are found to be good and have an acceptable level of internal consistency. Further, item total statistics is calculated to find out Cronbach's Alpha if item deleted. The variable with higher Cronbach's Alpha can be removed from the list. Table 4.2presents the value of Cronbach's Alpha if any item is deleted from the list.

Table 4.4: Item-Total Statistics

Items	Scale Mean if Item Deleted	Scale Variance if Item Deleted	Corrected Item-Total Correlation	Cronbach's Alpha if Item Deleted
1	123.25	93.575	0.024	0.881
2	123.29	92.679	0.105	0.877
3	123.30	90.911	0.223	0.871
4	123.47	91.649	0.208	0.872
5	123.38	92.063	0.148	0.875
6	123.91	91.250	0.163	0.874
7	123.62	91.491	0.180	0.873
8	123.40	90.714	0.214	0.871
9	123.48	90.633	0.219	0.871
10	123.43	89.970	0.324	0.866
11	123.50	90.696	0.206	0.871
12	123.28	91.903	0.173	0.873
13	123.26	91.975	0.169	0.874
14	123.27	91.741	0.185	0.873
15	123.34	93.500	0.026	0.881
16	123.43	90.035	0.243	0.869
17	123.46	91.136	0.157	0.874
18	123.41	93.058	0.043	0.881
19	123.43	92.718	0.071	0.879
20	123.48	89.977	0.237	0.869
21	123.44	91.383	0.160	0.874
22	123.24	94.091	0.090	0.882
23	123.25	93.425	0.039	0.880
24	123.29	92.722	0.089	0.878
25	123.38	91.596	0.152	0.874
26	123.44	90.436	0.231	0.870
27	123.34	91.864	0.146	0.875
28	123.40	92.624	0.083	0.878
29	124.43	78.180	0.385	0.851
30	125.44	70.102	0.531	0.826
31	125.39	70.439	0.506	0.831
32	126.24	75.811	0.398	0.850

Table 4.4 shows that removal of any item would result in excellent Cronbach's Alpha. All the 32 statements are greater than 0.9. The result clearly shows that there is no need to remove any item from the scale. Hence, it is concluded that there is a chance of applying factor analysis.

4.5. Attitude Level of the Respondents about Brand Management in Commercial Banks: Factor Analysis

The data collected for the study were classified, tabulated and processed for factor analysis, which is the most appropriate multivariate technique to identify the groups of determinants. Factor analysis identifies common dimensions of factors from the observed variables that link together the seemingly unrelated variables and provides insight into the underlying structure of the data. In this study, principal component analysis has been used since the objective is to summarize most of the information in a minimum number of factors for prediction purpose.

A principal component is a factor model in which the factors are based on the total variance. Another concept in factor analysis is the rotation of factors. Varimax rotations are one of the most popular methods used in the study to simplify the factor structure by maximizing the variance of a column of pattern matrix. Another technique called latent root criteria is used. An eigen value is the column sum of squares for a factor. It represents the amounts of variance in data. After determination of the common factors these are expressed as linear combinations of the observed variables.

Factor model: $F_i = W_{i1} + W_{i2} + \ldots \ldots W_{ik} * k$

Where Fi = estimate of the ith factor

                             Wi_1 = weight or factor score coefficient

                             K = number of variables.

A customer considers various factors while deciding about investing in a bank. Based on informal discussions with customers, all the relevant variables are included in the study. 32 statements are generated for measuring the attitude level of brand management in commercial banks on a five point scale. The factor analysis is conducted separately in all selected banks. Factor matrix and their corresponding factor loading after varimax rotation are presented in the given table.

Table 4.5: KMO and Bartlett's Testof Attitude Variables

Kaiser-Meyer-Olkin Measure of Sampling Adequacy.		0.692
Bartlett's Test of Sphericity	Approx. Chi-Square	8176.680
	DF	496

*Significant at 1% level

It is found from the Table 4.5 that the test value is 8176.680 at the level of 1% of significance. As the significance level is very small, it is clear that the correlation matrix is not an identity matrix. It proves that there exists correlation between the variables. It is also revealed that the value of test statistic is 0.692 which is more than 0.5. This indicates that the factor analysis for the selected variables is suitable for the data.

Table 4.6

Total Variance Attitude Variables								
Component	Initial Eigenvalues			Extraction Sums of Squared Loadings			Rotation Sums of Squared Loadings		
	Total	% of Variance	Cumulative %	Total	% of Variance	Cumulative %	Total	% of Variance	Cumulative %
1	3.591	11.223	11.223	3.591	11.223	11.223	2.977	9.302	9.302
2	3.282	10.255	21.478	3.282	10.255	21.478	2.930	9.156	18.458
3	2.954	9.230	30.708	2.954	9.230	30.708	2.843	8.884	27.342
4	2.584	8.076	38.784	2.584	8.076	38.784	2.577	8.054	35.396
5	2.275	7.111	45.894	2.275	7.111	45.894	2.137	6.679	42.075
6	1.577	4.927	50.822	1.577	4.927	50.822	1.931	6.034	48.109
7	1.416	4.426	55.248	1.416	4.426	55.248	1.587	4.959	53.068
8	1.332	4.163	59.411	1.332	4.163	59.411	1.489	4.652	57.720
9	1.159	3.623	63.034	1.159	3.623	63.034	1.443	4.509	62.229
10	1.062	3.317	66.351	1.062	3.317	66.351	1.319	4.122	66.351
11	0.992	3.099	69.450						
12	0.893	2.790	72.240						
13	0.787	2.459	74.699						
14	0.768	2.401	77.100						
15	0.750	2.345	79.445						
16	0.694	2.170	81.615						
17	0.663	2.072	83.686						
18	0.624	1.948	85.635						
19	0.594	1.856	87.491						
20	0.527	1.647	89.138						
21	0.506	1.582	90.720						
22	0.459	1.433	92.153						
23	0.435	1.359	93.513						
24	0.429	1.339	94.852						
25	0.359	1.121	95.973						
26	0.329	1.029	97.002						
27	0.326	1.020	98.022						
28	0.249	0.779	98.801						
29	0.171	0.536	99.336						
30	0.106	0.331	99.668						
31	0.064	0.201	99.868						
32	0.042	0.132	100.000						

Extraction Method: Principal Component Analysis.

Table 4.7

Rotated Component Matrix of Attitude Variables										
Component										
	1	2	3	4	5	6	7	8	9	10
Lack of Knowledge	**0.927**	-0.042	-0.011	0.044	-0.123	0.157	0.011	0.005	0.014	-0.029
I like to visit the website of my bank	**0.925**	-0.052	-0.017	0.030	-0.116	0.129	0.021	-0.006	0.045	-0.052
I am Compared to other people, I follow news about mybankvery closely	**0.827**	0.030	-0.055	-0.115	0.125	-0.115	0.036	0.042	0.082	-0.129
I would be interested in learning more about this bank	**0.665**	-0.003	0.126	0.037	-0.045	0.040	-0.064	0.024	-0.337	0.250
I have seriously considered changing my bank	0.040	**0.774**	0.060	-0.023	0.021	0.026	0.135	0.224	0.034	-0.051
I will possibly use this bank in the future	0.010	**0.764**	0.026	0.021	-0.027	-0.043	0.015	-0.051	-0.009	0.010
I have every intention of using this bank in the future	-0.014	**0.723**	0.005	-0.018	0.040	-0.020	0.043	0.222	0.032	-0.100
I will probably use this bank in the future	-0.023	**0.634**	-0.024	-0.003	-0.007	0.024	-0.126	0.128	0.015	0.129
I consider myself to be a loyal customer of this bank	-0.076	**0.596**	0.027	0.090	0.045	0.098	0.129	0.146	-0.020	-0.018
I will switch to a competitor bank when there are problems with this bank's service	0.002	0.027	**0.971**	0.031	0.024	0.000	0.003	0.018	-0.009	0.038
I will use other products/services offered by this bank in near future	0.012	-0.007	**0.966**	0.029	0.000	-0.016	0.067	-0.012	0.000	-0.013
I will switch to a competitor bank that offers more attractive benefits	-0.010	0.069	**0.954**	0.053	0.013	0.001	-0.034	-0.039	-0.009	0.020
My bank is Innovative	-0.003	0.003	0.018	**0.785**	0.023	0.006	-0.059	0.078	0.196	-0.191
Compared to other banks in this Industry, how well does your basic needs	0.087	0.032	0.021	**0.731**	-0.092	0.009	-0.064	0.071	0.056	0.333
Likeable	0.012	0.062	0.040	**0.719**	0.518	-0.103	0.039	-0.129	0.096	-0.011
Attractive benefits	-0.099	-0.021	0.079	**0.684**	-0.114	-0.104	0.104	0.039	-0.308	-0.141
I really love my bank	-0.136	0.131	-0.012	-0.069	**0.728**	0.069	-0.006	-0.140	0.217	0.290
I would really miss my bank if it went away	-0.026	-0.055	-0.004	-0.091	**0.725**	0.258	-0.030	0.115	-0.073	0.034
I can bank with this bank whenever i want	-0.011	-0.009	0.060	0.372	**0.666**	-0.063	-0.001	0.104	-0.251	-0.045
My bank is more then a bank to me	0.081	0.037	-0.057	-0.007	-0.020	**0.759**	-0.050	-0.018	0.251	-0.026
I really like to talk about this bank to others	0.082	0.159	0.018	-0.115	0.168	**0.677**	-0.118	-0.130	-0.041	-0.080
I am always interested in learning more about this bank	-0.050	-0.149	0.019	-0.083	0.144	**0.625**	0.130	0.277	-0.161	0.029
I really identify with people who bank with this bank	0.220	0.047	0.033	0.063	-0.123	**0.529**	-0.013	-0.090	-0.264	0.480
Overall I think this bank is a nice bank	0.028	0.099	0.003	-0.051	-0.017	-0.063	**0.778**	0.108	0.023	0.072
overall i think this bank is good	-0.033	-0.052	0.022	0.062	0.045	-0.018	**0.716**	-0.086	-0.003	-0.149
Overall I think this bank is desirable	0.054	0.373	0.002	-0.029	-0.112	0.049	**0.531**	0.054	0.001	0.275
I am likely to use this bank in the future	0.050	0.203	-0.021	0.070	0.026	0.028	-0.135	**0.640**	0.032	-0.144
Overall I think this bank is very attractive	0.010	0.332	0.073	0.003	0.088	-0.093	0.214	**0.588**	0.057	0.054
Overall I think this bank is extremely	-0.003	0.257	-0.066	-0.002	-0.047	0.040	0.040	**0.570**	0.023	0.145
I will recommend this bank to others	-0.018	0.003	0.012	0.046	-0.108	0.044	0.015	0.137	**0.884**	0.037
Trust worthy	-0.040	0.095	-0.023	0.461	0.296	-0.181	0.040	-0.212	**0.804**	0.006
Admirable	-0.136	-0.036	0.037	-0.090	0.328	-0.091	0.037	0.061	0.099	**0.750**

Extraction Method: Principal Component Analysis.

Rotation Method: Varimax with Kaiser Normalization.

Table 4.8: Statement Relating to Attitude Level of the Customers

Statements	Loadings	Factors
Lack of Knowledgeable	0.927	
I like to visit the website of my bank	0.925	
I am Compared to other people, I follow news about my bank very closely	0.827	Factor 1
I would be interested in learning more about this bank	0.665	
I have seriously considered changing my bank	0.774	
I will possibly use this bank in the future	0.764	
I have every intention of using this bank in the future	0.723	Factor 2
I will probably use this bank in the future	0.634	
I consider myself to be a loyal customer of this bank	0.596	
I will switch to a competitor bank when there are problems with this bank's service	0.971	
I will use other products/services offered by this bank in near future	0.966	Factor 3
I will switch to a competitor bank that offers more attractive benefits	0.954	
My bank is Innovative	0.785	
Compared to other banks in this Industry, how well doesyour basic needs	0.731	Factor 4
Likeable	0.719	
Attractive benefits	0.684	
I really love my bank	0.728	
I would really miss my bank if it went away	0.725	Factor 5
I can bank with this bank wheneverI want	0.666	
My bank is more than a bank to me	0.759	
I really like to talk about this bank to others	0.677	Factor 6
I am always interested in learning more about this bank	0.625	
I really identify with people who bank with this bank	0.529	
Overall I think this bank is a nice bank	0.778	
Overall I think this bank is good	0.716	Factor 7
Overall I think this bank is desirable	0.531	
I am likely to use this bank in the future	0.640	
Overall I think this bank is very attractive	0.588	Factor 8
Overall I think this bank is extremely extraordinary	0.570	
I will recommend this bank to others	0.884	
Trust worthy	0.804	Factor 9
Admirable	0.750	Factor 10

Table 4.8depicts the variables under each of the ten derived factors. The first factor comprises variables viz., Lack of Knowledge, I like to visit the website of my bank, I am compared to other people, I follow news about my bank very closely and I would be interested in learning more about this bank. These were grouped under factor F1 and termed as **'Brand Association'** represents the foundation for purchase intension (later developed into decision) and for brand loyalty. Brand association was all the brand-related thoughts, feeling, perceptions, images, etc… Therefore, brand association is everything customers' minds link to a certain brand. The key component of brand equity association is brand differentiation. When customers can easily identify unique characteristics in products or services, brand association is created.

The second factor includes the attributes such as I have seriously considered changing my bank, I will possibly use this bank in the future, I have every intention of using this bank in the future, I will probably use this bank in the future and I consider myself to be a loyal customer of this bank. This factor can be termed as **'Brand Performance'**. Brand Performance is the capability that the product or service has to meet the customers' expectations and functional needs.

The third factor includes the attributes such as I will switch to a competitor bank when there are problems with this bank's service, I will use other products/services offered by this bank in near future and I will switch to a competitor bank that offers more attractive benefits. This factor can be termed as **'Brand Environment'**.

The fourth factor includes the attributes such as My bank is Innovative, Compared to other banks in this Industry, how well does your basic needs, Likeable and Attractive benefits. These were grouped under F4 and termed as **'Brand Feeling'**. Brand feelings are representations of the customer emotional response to the brand and the intrinsic value consumers have from the brand.

The fifth factor includes the attributes such as I really love my bank, I would really miss my bank if it went away and I can bank with this bank whenever I want. These were grouped under factor F5 and termed as **'Brand Judgment'**. Brand judgments are the reflections of the customers' personal opinions and evaluations towards a specific brand.

The sixth factor includes the attributes such as My bank is more then a bank to me, I really like to talk about this bank to others, I am always interested in learning more about this bank and I really identify with people who bank with this bank. These were grouped under F6 and termed as **'Brand Image'**. Brand Imagery refers to the extrinsic properties of the product or service.

The seventh factor includes the attributes such as Overall I think this bank is a nice bank, Overall I think this bank is good and Overall I think this bank is desirable. These were grouped under factor F7 and termed as **'Brand Quality'**. Brand quality is consumers' general beliefs over a product quality comparing to competitive brands.

The eighth factor includes the attributes such as I am likely to use this bank in the future, Overall I think this bank is very attractive and Overall I think this bank is extremely. This factor can be termed as **'Brand Loyalty'**.

The ninth factor includes the attributes such as I will recommend this bank to others and Trust worthy. These were grouped under F4 and termed as **'Brand Resonance'**. Brand resonance is the relation consumers and brands share which includes the willingness to purchase, as well as the will to recommend the product or service. The tenth factor include the attributes Admirable.

4.6. Summary

In this chapter, customer attitude level of brand management in commercial banks. To examine the attitude level, necessary primary data are gathered using questionnaire method. For which, 32 relevant statements have been prearranged in the questionaire by using Rensis Likert's 5 point rating scale technique. Such collected data have been calculated with the help of various statistical tools like Chi-square test, the reliability of statements used to calculate the attitude level has been tested by using Cronbach's Alpha Reliability Analysis. The attitude statements comprised and arranged into a meaningful set using Factor Analysis.

Regarding Chi square test in private sector banks, there is an association between demographic variables viz., Age, Gender, Educational Qualification, Marital Status, Occupation, Annual Income, Total Experience of the respondents and the satisfaction level towards brand management. There is no significant association between Educational Qualification and Total Experience and the satisfaction level towards brand management.

In Public sector banks, the chi square test reveals that there is an association between demographic variables like Age, Gender, Educational Qualification, Marital Status, Occupation, Annual Income, Total Experience of the respondents and the satisfaction level towards brand management. There is no significant association between Occupation and Total Experience and the satisfaction level towards brand management.

From the Cronbach's Alpha reliability test, it is noted that the factors used to examine the attitude level of the sample respondents about the customer are reliable and have an acceptable point of internal consistency.

Principal component analysis was used since the objective is to summarize most of the original information in a minimum number of factors for prediction purpose.

Varimax rotations were used in the study to simplify the factor structure by maximizing the variance of a column of pattern matrix. An Eigen value is the column sum of squares for a factor represents the amount of variance in data. After determination of the common factors, factors scores were estimated for each factor. The common factor themselves were expressed as linear combinations of the observed variables.

In Factor Analysis, 32 statements used to test the attitude level of the sample customer about the scheme have been grouped into 10 factors viz., Brand Association, Brand Performance, Brand Environment, Brand Feeling, Brand Judgment, Brand Image, Brand Quality, Brand Loyalty, Brand Resonance and Brand admirable.

CHAPTER V

CUSTOMERS' SATISFACTION TOWARDS BRAND MANAGEMENT

IN COMMERCIAL BANKS

5.1.   Introduction

In India, commercial banks play a very important role and are the largest part of financial institution. The banking industry in India is become more integrated due to the technological environment, liberalization and deregulation. As a result, the market environment in banking sector has become more competitive and complex. The banking product currently very much homogeneous from one bank to another bank and at the same time the demand from bank customers are keep on increasing where banks need to do more effective industry transformation. Banks previously emphasized on their products are gradually shifted to be more customer focus which is parallel with the relational marketing principle where customer loyalty will be the main focus.

In this view, the branding is particularly important to the financial sector in the current economy, since investors and other big spenders are being cautious about making large financial transactions. Structurally, bank brands are handicapped in that they cannot be illustrated. For banks today, the strength and marketing power of an institution's brand is rapidly becoming one of the critical levers for differentiation and success.

Banks need to provide a consistent brand experience to prevent customers from switching to rival banks. Hence, the field of bank service is now emphasizing the importance of customer-oriented marketing.

Banks endeavour to establish marketing strategies which promote brand image among customers for enhancing the satisfaction and loyalty of customers as well as further promoting performance.

The sequence of customer satisfaction in reference to satisfied customers, delighted customers and loyal customers can be expressed in chart 1.

Customer Satisfaction for Better Performance

In the present scenario, successful corporations gain competitive advantage through increased efficiency, high quality of service and improved customer relationship. Customers get information about the organization through customer advocacy. Creating and maintaining customer loyalty have become important in current service markets. In financial service industry, maintaining superior service quality is considered critical in achieving customer satisfaction, value creation and growth. The ability to understand the needs of the consumer with respect to the product or service is vital for measuring the level of consumer satisfaction. Every business organization aims to satisfy its customers to a great extent, as the customer satisfaction lays foundation for the success of the business. The measurement of customer satisfaction has become mandatory in any organization. The quality of the products or the quality of customer service determines the degree of customer satisfaction. The customer satisfaction not only means, satisfying the customers but also customer retention in case of service failure. The organization should solve the complaints through various service recovery strategies. It is mandatory to identify the impact of service failure and customer feedback for the survival, success and prosperity of an organization. The real victory of an organization is based on the degree of loyalty of the customers. The measurement of customer satisfaction is intricate because most of the customers do not believe in the act of complaining as they feel it to be a waste of time and effort. Some of the customers may indulge in negative word-of-mouth, which will have a severe impact on the turnover of the organization. To avoid the negative impact on the revenue, every organization must collect feedback from its own customers. They should study and analyze the existing system of customer service and implement continuous improvement strategies by enhancing the quality of the service. The achievement of a high degree of banking customer satisfaction and loyalty represents an important field for brand management.

The Need to Measure Customer Satisfaction

Satisfied customers are central to optimal performance and financial returns. In many places in the world, business organizations have been elevating the role of the customer to that of a key stakeholder over the past twenty years. Customers are viewed as a group whose satisfaction with the enterprise must be incorporated in strategic planning efforts. Forward-looking companies are finding value in directly measuring and tracking customer satisfaction (CS) as an important strategic success indicator. Evidence is mounting that placing a high priority on CS is critical to improved organizational performance in a global marketplace.

With better understanding of customers' Satisfactions, companies can determine the actions required to meet the customers' needs. They can identify their own strengths and weaknesses, where they stand in comparison to their competitors, chart out path future progress and improvement. Customer satisfaction measurement helps to promote an increased focus on customer outcomes and stimulate improvements in the work practices and processes used within the company.

When buyers are powerful, the health and strength of the company's relationship with its customers – its most critical economic asset – is its best predictor of the future. Assets on the balance sheet – basically assets of production – are good predictors only when buyers are weak. So it is no wonder that the relationship between those assets and future income is becoming more and more tenuous. As buyers become empowered, sellers have no choice but to adapt. Focusing on competition has its place, but with buyer power on the rise, it is more important to pay attention to the customer.

It is fact that the satisfaction level of the customers is an important fact for the success of any bank and the strategies adopted by them. Customers' satisfaction level denotes the highlights reached by the banks. Hence, it becomes inevitable to analyse the satisfaction of the customers. Against this background, this chapter is a modest attempt to examine the satisfaction level of the customers brand management in commercial banking. On the basis of discussion and deliberations with the bank customers, academic experts, bank officials and also based on the review of relevant literature, a list of 19 statements has been prepared to identify the level of satisfaction of the brand management in commercial banking. Required primary data have been collected from the selected 580 sample customers. Such collected data have been analysed with the help of various statistical tools like Chi-square test, 'F' test, 'Z' test and Contingency Co-efficient at 5% level of significance. Further, Cronbach's Alpha Reliability test, Multiple Regression Analysis and Factor analysis have also been applied.

5.2. Quantification of Data and Measurement of Satisfaction Level of the Customers

To analyse the customers' towards brand management in commercial banks, the required primary data have been collected by using a list of 22 statements. On the basis of outcome of the pilot study and by using item analysis techniques, two statements have been dropped. Finally, 20 statements are identified as significant and the same have been used in the final questionnaire for data collection, using Rensis Likert's 5 point rating scale ranging from 'highly satisfaction' to 'highly dissatisfaction'. If a customer has highly satisfaction with the statement, a scale value of 5 is assigned, scale value of 4 is assigned, if the response is satisfaction, 3 if the customer is average, 2 if the customers satisfaction is dissatisfied and 1 if the satisfaction is highly dissatisfied. The total score for each sample customer from all 19 statements are calculated by using the above scoring procedure.

An individual's score is mere summation of scores secured from 19 statements of each sample customer. The scores of the sample customers range from 19 statements of each sample customer. The scores of the sample customers range from 19 to 95. The average score is 57. Based on the average score, the sample customers have been grouped in to two categories viz., low satisfaction (whose score is less than 57) and high satisfaction (whose score is between 58 and 114). Classification of the sample customers on the basis of their satisfaction score is presented in Table 5.1.

Table 5.1: Distribution of Sample Customers Based on Level of Satisfaction

Satisfaction	Number of Customers	Per cent	Average Score	S. D
Private sector banks				
Low Level	318	54.8	56.57	8.56
High Level	66	11.4	79.36	5.39
Total	384	66.2	60.49	11.82
Public sector banks				
Low Level	168	29.0	56.80	8.45
High Level	28	4.8	79.89	6.15
Total	196	33.8	60.10	11.48

Figures in parentheses are percentage

Table 5.1 shows that the private sector banks majority (54.8%) of the sample customers is having low level satisfaction about their banks and brand management. The average score is 56.57 and standard deviation is 8.56. In the case of public sector banks majority (29.0%) of the sample customers are having low level satisfaction about their banks and brand management. The average score is 56.80 and standard deviation is 8.45.

5.3. Relationship between the Independent Variables and Satisfaction Level

It is expected that the independent variables of the sample customers would influence the satisfaction level of the customers about their banks and brand management. To examine the association between the satisfaction level and independent variables, the following null hypothesis has been framed.

H_o: There is no significant association between the independent variables (age, gender, educational qualification, marital status, occupation and annual income) of the sample customers and their customer satisfaction towards brand management in commercial banks.

This hypothesis has been tested with Chi-square test, 'F' test, 'Z' test and Contingency Co-efficient(C) at 1% level of significance.

5.3.1. Age and Satisfaction Level

Age plays an essential role in determining the satisfaction level of customers. The respondents were classified as follows: Group A: 18-30 years; Group B: 31-50 years and Group C: Above 50 years.

To test the hypothesis which states that the customers' satisfaction level under different age groups does not differ significantly, Chi-square test was applied.

Table 5.2: Age And Satisfaction Level: χ^2Test

Private Sector	Level of Satisfaction		Total
Age Group	Low Level	High Level	
18 - 30 years(A)	81(83.5)	16(16.4)	97(100)
31-50 years(B)	200(81.3)	46(18.6)	246(100)
Above 50 years(C)	37(90.2)	4(9.7)	41(100)
Total	318(82.8)	66(17.1)	384(100)
Chi-square value =2.018			
Public Sector	**Level of Satisfaction**		**Total**
Age Group	Low Level	High Level	
18 - 30 years(A)	64(85.3)	11(14.6)	75(100)
31-50 years(B)	74(85.0)	13(14.9)	87(100)
Above 50 years(C)	30(88.2)	4(11.7)	34(100)
Total	168(85.7)	28(14.2)	196(100)
Chi-square value =0.216			

Figures in parentheses are percentage

It is evident from the table 5.2, the private and public sector banks respondents who are at the age of C category low level satisfaction compared to other age groups.

In the case of Private sector (2.018) and Public sector (0.216) banks, the calculated value of chi-square is less than the table value (6.634) at 1% level of significance. Therefore, it is inferred that there is no significant association between the age of the respondents and level of satisfaction.

Average Satisfaction Scores of Customers on the Basis of Age

The average attitude score of the three groups of respondents classified based on their age is given in the table 5.3.

Table 5.3: Age and Satisfaction Score

Private Sector Age Group	Number of Customers	Total Score	Average Score
18 - 30 years(A)	97(16.7)	5789	59.68
31-50 years(B)	246(42.4)	14960	60.81
Above 50 years(C)	14(7.1)	2480	60.48
Total	384(66.2)	23229	66.49
Public Sector Age Group	Number of Customers	Total Score	Average Score
18 - 30 years(A)	75(12.9)	4522	60.29
31-50 years(B)	87(15.0)	5236	60.18
Above 50 years(C)	34(5.9)	2023	59.50
Total	196(33.8)	11781	60.10

Figures in parentheses are percentage

It is clear from Table 5.3, in the case of private sector banks average score (60.81) of the B category is found to be higher than that of other two groups. In the case of public sector banks average score (60.29) of the A category is found to be higher than that of other two groups. The test of significance is applied to find out the significance of relationship between the average score of the sample customers belonging to different age group and satisfaction. Hence 'F' test is applied, the results are presented in Table 5.4.

Table 5.4: Age and Satisfaction Level: 'F' Test

Source of Variation	Sum of Square	Df	Mean Square	'F' Value	Result
Between Samples	64.665	2	32.332	0.235	Insignificant
Within Samples	79247.301	577	137.344		
Total	79311.966	579			

It is evident from the Table 5.4 that the calculated value (0.235) does not exceed the table value for 2 degrees of freedom. Hence, the framed null hypothesis was accepted and it can be concluded that there is a association in the average score of the sample customers belonging to different age groups.

5.3.2. Gender and Satisfaction Level

There may be variation in the level of satisfaction depending upon the gender of sample customers. To test the hypothesis that the level of satisfaction of different groups of the respondents classified based on their gender does not differ significantly, chi-square test was applied. The findings regarding the gender and satisfaction level of the sample customers are shown in Table 5.5.

Table 5.5: Gender And Satisfaction Level: χ^2Test

Private Sector	Level of Satisfaction		Total
Gender	Low Level	High Level	
Male	193(85.0)	34(14.9)	227(100)
Female	125(79.6)	32(20.3)	157(100)
Total	318(82.8)	66(17.1)	384(100)
Chi-square value = 1.904			
Public Sector	Level of Satisfaction		Total
Gender	Low Level	High Level	
Male	70(88.6)	9(11.3)	79(100)
Female	98(83.7)	19(16.2)	117(100)
Total	168(85.7)	28(14.2)	196(100)
Chi-square value = 0.905			

Figures in parentheses are percentage

Table 5.5 shows that out of 384 respondents belongs to private sector, 85% of the male customers and 79.6% of female customers opined that their level of satisfaction was low. Out of 196 respondents belongs to public sector banks, 88.6% of male customers and 83.7% of female customers are at low level satisfaction.

Both in Private sector (1.904) and Public sector (0.905) banks, the calculated values of chi-square are less than the table value (6.634) at 1 % level of significance. Therefore, it is inferred that there is no significant association between the gender of the respondents and level of Satisfaction.

Average Satisfaction Scores of Customers on the Basis of Gender

The average attitude score of the two groups of respondents classified based on their gender is presented in the table 5.6.

Table 5.6: Gender and Satisfaction Score

Private Sector Gender	Number of Customers	Total Score	Average Score
Male	227(39.1)	13444	59.22
Female	157(27.1)	9785	62.32
Total	384(66.2)	23229	60.49
Public Sector Gender	Number of Customers	Total Score	Average Score
Male	79(13.6)	7076	59.55
Female	117(20.2)	4705	60.47
Total	196(33.8)	11781	60.10

Figures in parentheses are percentage

The average satisfaction score of the two groups of respondents classified based on their gender is given in table 5.6. It shows that the average satisfaction score of the male in private sector (59.22) is lower than the average satisfaction score of female category(62.32). The average satisfaction score of the male group in public sector (59.55) is lower than the average satisfaction score of female group (60.47). To test the hypothesis, which states that satisfaction score of the customer based on their gender is the same, 'Z' test was applied. Details of the findings are presented in Table 5.7.

Table 5.7: Gender and Satisfaction Level: 'Z' Test

Private sector	Mean I $\overline{X_1}$	Mean II $\overline{X_2}$	MD $|\overline{X_1}-\overline{X_2}|$	SD	'Z' Value	Result
	1	2	3	4	5(3÷4)	Insignificant
	59.22	62.32	-3.1	0.745	0.186	
Public sector	Mean I $\overline{X_1}$	Mean II $\overline{X_2}$	MD $|\overline{X_1}-\overline{X_2}|$	SD	'Z' Value	Result
	1	2	3	4	5(3÷4)	Insignificant
	59.55	60.47	-0.92	0.493	1.866	

Table 5.7 shows that the calculated 'Z' value of private sector banks (0.186) and public sector banks (1.866) is less than the Table value (1.96). Hence, it can be concluded that there is no significant difference in the mean scores of the two categories based on the gender of the sample customers.

5.3.3. *Marital Status and Satisfaction Level*

A person's satisfaction level may vary according to marital status. The satisfaction of the married respondents would be higher than the unmarried respondents. Normally, the bachelor respondents, with less social responsibility, have less satisfaction about the banking sectors. It is decided to analyze the relationship between the marital status of the sample respondents and their level of satisfaction. Hence, in order to test the association between the marital status and satisfaction level, the sample customers are grouped into 2 categories viz., Married and Unmarried. The findings are shown in Table 5.8.

Table 5.8: Marital Status and Satisfaction Level: χ^2Test

Private Sector	Level of Satisfaction		Total
Marital status	Low Level	High Level	
Married	231(82.2)	50(17.7)	281(100)
Unmarried	87(84.4)	16(15.5)	103(100)
Total	318(82.8)	66(17.1)	384(100)
Chi-square value = 0.270			
Public Sector	Level of Satisfaction		Total
Marital status	Low Level	High Level	
Married	101(84.8)	18(15.1)	126(100)
Unmarried	67(87.0)	10(12.9)	70(100)
Total	164(85.7)	28(14.2)	196(100)
Chi-square value = 0.172			

Figures in parentheses are percentage

It is evident from the table 5.8 that the sample unmarried customer of both private sector banks (84.4) and public sector banks (87%) are having low satisfaction. It is also clear that (82.2%) of the sample married customer of private sector banks are 84.8% of sample married customers of public sector banks are having low satisfaction.

The calculated value is both public sector banks and private sector banks are less than the table value. The framed null hypothesis is accepted. Therefore, it can be concluded that there is no significant association between the marital status and satisfaction level of the sample customers.

Average Satisfaction Scores of Customers on the Basis of Marital Status

The average attitude score of the two groups of respondents classified based on their marital status is presented in the table 5.9.

Table 5.9: Marital Status and Satisfaction Score

Private Sector Marital status	Number of Customers	Total Score	Average Score
Married	281(48.4)	17074	60.76
Unmarried	103(17.8)	6155	59.75
Total	384(66.2)	23229	60.49
Public Sector Marital status	Number of Customers	Total Score	Average Score
Married	126(21.7)	7548	59.90
Unmarried	70(12.1)	4233	60.47
Total	196(33.8)	11781	60.10

Figures in parentheses are percentage

The average satisfaction score of the two groups of customers based on their marital status is presented in table 5.9. It indicates that the average satisfaction score of the customers belonging to married customers (60.76) of private sector was higher than that of unmarried customers (59.75). The average satisfaction score of the customers belonging to unmarried customers (60.47) of public sector was higher than that of married customers (59.90). It was proposed to test the hypothesis that the average score of married customer and unmarried customers is the same. Hence 'Z' test is applied which is shown in Table 5.10.

Table 5.10: Marital Status and Satisfaction Level: 'Z' Test

Private sector	Mean I $\overline{X_1}$	Mean II $\overline{X_2}$	MD $|X_1\text{-}X_2|$	SD	'Z' Value	Result
	1	2	3	4	5(3÷4)	Insignificant
	60.76	59.75	1.01	11.82	0.085	
Public sector	Mean I $\overline{X_1}$	Mean II $\overline{X_2}$	MD $|X_1\text{-}X_2|$	SD	'Z' Value	Result
	1	2	3	4	5(3÷4)	Insignificant
	59.90	60.47	-0.57	11.48	0.049	

Table 5.10 shows that the calculated 'Z' value of private sector (0.085) and a public sector bank (0.049) is less than the Table value. Hence, it can be concluded that there is no significant difference in the mean scores of the two categories based on the marital status of the sample customers.

5.3.4. *Educational Level and Satisfaction Level*

It is decided to analyze the relationship between the educational qualification of the respondents and their level of satisfaction. Table 5.11 gives information regarding the educational qualification of the respondents and their level of satisfaction. It is proposed to test the hypothesis that the customer's opinion about the satisfaction of the different groups of respondents classified based on the educational qualification does not differ significantly. Chi-square test is applied. For the purpose of analysis, the sample customers are grouped into 4 categories viz., No formal education, School level, UG level and PG & above. The details of the findings are highlighted in Table 5.11.

Table 5.11: Educational Qualification and Satisfaction Level: χ^2Test

Private Sector	Level of Satisfaction		Total
Educational qualification	Low Level	High Level	
No Formal Education	31(77.5)	9(22.5)	40(100)
School Level	96(80.6)	23(19.3)	119(100)
UG Level	121(82.8)	25(17.1)	146(100)
PG &Above	70(88.6)	9(11.3)	79(100)
Total	318(82.8)	66(17.1)	384(100)
Chi-square value = 3.041			

Public Sector	Level of Satisfaction		Total
Educational qualification	Low Level	High Level	
No Formal Education	18(85.7)	3(14.2)	21(100)
School Level	55(83.3)	11(16.6)	66(100)
UG Level	64(86.4)	10(13.5)	74(100)
PG &Above	31(88.5)	4(11.4)	35(100)
Total	168(85.7)	28(14.2)	96(100)
Chi-square value = 0.575			

Figures in parentheses are percentage

With regard to customers level of satisfaction, table 5.11 indicates that the percentage is continuously increasing from 'A' group to 'D' group. It means that educational level indicates the dissatisfaction also increases correspondingly.

In the case of private sector (3.041) and public sector (0.575) banks, the calculated value of Chi-square is less than the table value (11.344). The framed null hypothesis is accepted. Therefore, it can be concluded that there is no significant association between the Educational qualification and satisfaction level of the sample customers.

Average Satisfaction Scores of Customers on the Basis of Educational Qualification

The average attitude score of the four groups of respondents classified based on their educational qualification is presented in the table 5.12.

Table 5.12: Educational Qualification and Satisfaction Score

Private Sector Educational qualification	Number of Customers	Total Score	Average Score
No Formal education	40(6.9)	2484	62.10
School Level	119(20.5)	7259	61.00
UG Level	146(25.2)	8937	61.21
PG &Above	79(13.6)	4549	57.58
Total	384(66.2)	23229	60.49
Public Sector Educational qualification	Number of Customers	Total Score	Average Score
No Formal education	21(3.6)	1244	62.10
School Level	66(11.4)	3971	60.16
UG Level	74(12.8)	4538	61.32
PG &Above	35(6.0)	2028	57.94
Total	196(33.8)	11781	60.10

Figures in parentheses are percentage

The average satisfaction score of the two groups of sample customers based on their educational qualification is given in table 5.12. The table indicates that the average score of the respondents belonging to A group (62.10) of private sector banks is higher than the group B (61.00), group C (61.21) and group D (57.58). In public sector banks also the average score of respondents belonging to group A (62.10) is higher than the group B (60.16), group C (61.32) and group D (57.94). It was proposed to test hypothesis that the average score of two groups of customers based on educational qualification is the same. For this purpose, 'F' test was applied which is shown in table 5.13.

Table 5.13: Educational Qualification and Satisfaction Level: 'F' Test

Source of Variation	Sum of Square	Df	Mean Square	'F' Value	Result
Between Samples	1041.616	3	347.205	2.555	Insignificant
Within Samples	78270.350	576	135.886		
Total	79311.966	579			

Table 5.13 highlights that the calculated value of 'F' is 2.555 which is less than the Theoretical value of 3.78. Hence, the framed null hypothesis is accepted and it can be concluded that the no association between the mean score of the sample customers with different level of education and Satisfaction level is found to be insignificant.

5.3.5. *Occupational Status and Satisfaction Level*

The satisfaction level of the people may vary according to their occupational status. An attempt is made to examine the association between the occupational status and satisfaction level of the sample customers. For this purpose, the sample customers are grouped into 5 categories viz., Business, Employed, Agricultural, Student/Housewife and pensioner. The distribution of the sample customers according to their occupational status and satisfaction level is shown in Table 5.14.

Table 5.14: Occupational Status and Satisfaction Level: χ^2Test

Private Sector	Level of Satisfaction		Total
Occupational status	Low Level	High Level	
Business	55(83.3)	11(16.6)	66(100)
Employed	105(79.5)	27(20.4)	132(100)
Agricultural	92(83.6)	18(16.3)	110(100)
Student/Housewife	59(92.1)	5(7.8)	64(100)
Pensioner	7(58.3)	5(41.6)	12(100)
Total	318(82.8)	66(17.1)	383(100)
Chi-square value = 2.860			
Public Sector	**Level of Satisfaction**		**Total**
Occupational status	**Low Level**	**High Level**	
Business	45(78.9)	12(21.0)	57(100)
Employed	46(92.0)	4(8.0)	50(100)
Agricultural	53(85.4)	9(14.5)	62(100)
Student/Housewife	12(85.7)	2(14.2)	14(100)
Pensioner	12(92.3)	1(7.6)	13(100)
Total	168(85.7)	28(14.2)	196(100)
Chi-square value =4.209			

Figures in parentheses are percentage

From the Table 5.14 it is evident that in case of private sector 92.1% of the D category have low satisfactory rates followed other sample customers while in case of public sector 92.3% of the E category have low satisfactory rates compared to other sample customers.

The calculated value of private sector (2.860) and public sector (4.209) banks is less than the Table value (11.344). The framed null hypothesis is accepted. Therefore, it can be concluded that there is no significant association between the occupational status and satisfaction level of the sample customers.

Average Satisfaction Scores of Customers on the Basis of Occupational Status

The average attitude score of the four groups of respondents classified based on their occupational status is presented in the table 5.15.

Table 5.15: Occupational Status and Satisfaction Score

Private Sector Occupational status	Number of Customers	Total Score	Average Score
Business	66(11.4)	3951	59.86
Employed	132(22.8)	7977	60.43
Agricultural	110(19.0)	6682	60.74
Student/Housewife	69(11.9)	4222	61.18
Pensioner	7(1.2)	397	59.7
Total	384(66.2)	23229	60.49
Public Sector **Occupational status**	**Number of Customers**	**Total Score**	**Average Score**
Business	57(9.8)	3533	61.98
Employed	50(8.6)	2841	56.82
Agricultural	62(10.7)	3748	60.45
Student/Housewife	14(2.4)	886	63.28
Pensioner	13(2.2)	773	59.46
Total	196(33.8)	11781	60.10

Figures in parentheses are percentage

The average satisfaction score of the two groups of sample customers based on their educational qualification is given in table 5.15. The table indicates that the average score of the respondents belonging to D group (61.18) of private sector banks is higher than the group C (60.74), group B (60.47), group A (59.86) and group E (59.70). In public sector banks also the average score of respondents belonging to group D (63.28) is higher than the group A (61.98), group C (60.45), group E (59.46) and group B (56.82). It was proposed to test hypothesis that the average score of two groups of customers based on occupational status is the same. For this purpose, 'F' test was applied which is shown in table 5.16.

Table 5.16: Occupational Status and Satisfaction Level: 'F' Test

Source of Variation	Sum of Square	Df	Mean Square	'F' Value	Result
Between Samples	381.812	4	95.453	0.695	Insignificant
Within Samples	78930.154	575	137.270		
Total	79311.966	579			

Table 5.16 shows that the calculated value (0.695) of 'F' is less than the Theoretical value (3.78). Thus, it can be concluded that the no association between the mean score of the sample customers and satisfaction level is found to be insignificant.

5.3.6. *Annual Income and Satisfaction Level*

Income will influence the life style of the people. Income of the sample customers may also determine their satisfaction level. Hence, the annual income is another essential one to assess the satisfaction level. The satisfaction level of the customers in different annual income group may vary. Based on their annual family income, the sample customers are classified into three groups viz., (Up to Rs.2,00,000), (Rs.2,00,001 to Rs.5,00,000) and(Above Rs.5,00,000). The details of the findings are shown in the Table 5.17.

Table 5.17: Annual Income Status Satisfaction Level: χ^2Test

Private Sector	Level of Satisfaction		Total
Annual income	Low Level	High Level	
Up to Rs.2,00,000	161(83.4)	32(16.5)	193(100)
Rs 2,00,001 to Rs.5,00,000	124(81.5)	28(18.4)	152(100)
Above Rs.5,00,000	33(84.6)	6(15.3)	39(100)
Total	318(82.8)	66(17.1)	384(100)
Chi-square value = 0.302			
Public Sector	**Level of Satisfaction**		**Total**
Annual income	**Low Level**	**High Level**	
Up to Rs.2,00,000	75(80.6)	18(19.3)	93(100)
Rs 2,00,001 to Rs.5,00,000	73(90.1)	8(9.8)	81(100)
Above Rs. 5,00,000	20(90.9)	2(9.0)	22(100)
Total	168(8.7)	28(14.2)	196(100)
Chi-square value = 3.722			

Figures in parentheses are percentage

Table 5.17 shows that, in the case of private sector & public sector banks, group C customers are having low level Satisfaction about brand management. Both in private sector and public sector banks, the calculated value of Chi-square is less than the Table value. The framed null hypothesis is accepted. Therefore, it can be concluded that there is no significant association between the Annual income and Satisfaction level of the sample customers.

Average Satisfaction Scores of Customers on the Basis of Annual Income

The average attitude score of the three groups of respondents classified based on their annual income is presented in the table 5.18.

Table 5.18: Annual Income and Satisfaction Score

Private Sector Annual income	Number of Customers	Total Score	Mean Score
Up to Rs. 2,00,000	193(33.3)	11607	60.13
Rs 2,00,001 to Rs.5,00,000	152(26.2)	5849	60.94
Above Rs.5,00,000	39(6.7)	2359	60.48
Total	384(66.2)	23229	60.49
Public Sector Annual income	Number of Customers	Total Score	Mean Score
Up to Rs.2,00,000	93(16.0)	9263	62.89
Rs 2,00,001 to Rs. 5,00,000	81(14.0)	4658	57.50
Above Rs. 5,00,000	22(3.8)	1274	57.90
Total	196(33.8)	11781	60.10

Figures in parentheses are percentage

The average satisfaction score of the three groups of respondents classified based on their annual income is given in table 5.18. It shows that the average satisfaction score of the category B in private sector banks (60.94) is higher than the other groups in private sector banks. The average satisfaction score of the category A customer in public sector banks (62.89) is higher than the other groups in public sector banks. To test the hypothesis, which states that satisfaction score of the customer based on their annual income is the same, 'F' test was applied. Details of the findings are presented in Table 5.19.

Table 5.19: Annual Income and Satisfaction Level: 'F' Test

Source of Variation	Sum of Square	Df	Mean Square	'F' Value	Result
Between Samples	151.985	2	30.397	0.220	Insignificant
Within Samples	79159.980	574	137.909		
Total	79311.966	579			

It is evident from the Table 5.19 that the calculated value (0.220) of 'F' is less than the Theoretical value (4.60). Therefore, it can be concluded that the no association between the mean score of the sample customers on the basis of their annual income and Satisfaction level of the sample customers is found to be insignificant.

5.4. Satisfaction Level of the Respondents about the Brand Management in Commercial Banks: Reliability Test- Cronbach's Alpha

The required primary data collected from the sample respondents in order to measure the satisfactory level of the respondents about brand management in commercial banking are collected through 5 point Likert's scale technique using 19 relevant statements. The validity of the statements is measured through Reliability analysis. Cronbach's Alpha is the most common measure of internal consistency[1]. In the present study, the reliability analysis is applied to measure the reliability and internal consistency of the variables used to measure the satisfaction level. The reliability statistics provides the actual value for Cronbach's Alpha. It is shown in Table 5.20.

Table 5.20: Reliability Statistics: Cronbach's Alpha

Cronbach's Alpha	Number of Items
0.866	19

It is clear from the Table 5.20that the calculated value of Cronbach's Alpha is 0.866 for 19 items used for the analysis. The value is below the suitable range (ie., between 0.80 and 0.90). Therefore, it can be concluded that the factors used to measure the satisfaction level are found to be reliable and have an acceptable level of internal consistency.

Further, item total statistics is calculated to find out Cronbach's Alpha if item is deleted. The variable with higher Cronbach's Alpha can be removed from the list. Table 5.2 presents the value of Cronbach's Alpha if any item is deleted from the list.

Table 5.21: Item-Total Statistics

Items	Scale Mean if Item Deleted	Scale Variance if Item Deleted	Corrected Item-Total Correlation	Cronbach's Alpha if Item Deleted
1	74.95	48.699	0.414	0.862
2	75.16	50.144	0.372	0.863
3	75.24	48.015	0.582	0.855
4	75.34	49.515	0.477	0.859
5	75.30	49.355	0.468	0.860
6	75.86	49.782	0.343	0.864
7	75.54	48.463	0.493	0.858
8	75.35	47.485	0.542	0.856
9	75.38	47.045	0.605	0.854
10	75.31	47.559	0.652	0.853
11	75.10	48.615	0.428	0.861
12	75.02	49.571	0.420	0.861
13	75.18	49.166	0.453	0.860
14	75.31	48.704	0.509	0.858
15	75.31	49.311	0.470	0.859
16	75.62	49.683	0.325	0.866
17	75.62	49.618	0.365	0.863
18	75.39	48.387	0.477	0.859
19	75.34	47.544	0.544	0.856

Table 5.21 shows that removal of any item would result in good internal consistency of Cronbach's Alpha. All the 19 statements are greater than 0.8. The result clearly shows that there is no need to remove any item from the scale. Hence, it is concluded that there is a chance of applying factor analysis.

---

[1] https://stastistics.laerd.com/cronbachs-alpha-using-spss.statistics.php, retrieved on 12.05.2015.

5.5. Satisfaction Level of the Respondents about the Brand Management in Commercial Banks-Factor Analysis

Table 5.22: KMO and Barlett's Test of Satisfaction Variables

Kaiser-Meyer-Olkin Measure of Sampling Adequacy.		0.720
Bartlett's Test of Sphericity	Approx. Chi-Square	5067.69
	Df	171
	Significance	0.000

*Significant at 1% level

It is found from the Table 5.22 that the test value is 5067.69 at 1% level of significance. As the significance level is smaller, it is found that the correlation matrix is not an identity matrix. It entails that there is a correlation between the variables. It is also revealed that the value of test statistic is 0.720 which is more than 0.5. This proves that the factor analysis for the selected variables is suitable to the data. The Principal Component Analysis has been applied to extract the factors since the objective is to summarize most of the original information into a minimum number of factors for prediction purpose. A Principal Component Analysis is a factor model used to convert a set of correlated factors into a set of uncorrelated factors so that the factors are unrelated and variables selected for each factor are related. The variance extracted by the factors is called Eigen values. The total variance by successive factors is shown in Table 5.23.

Table 5.23: Total Variance of Satisfaction Variables

Component	Initial Eigen Values			Extraction Sums of Squared Loadings		
	Total	% of Variance	Cumulative %	Total	% of Variance	Cumulative %
1	5.762	30.325	30.325	5.762	30.325	30.325
2	2.340	12.315	42.639	2.340	12.315	42.639
3	1.584	8.339	50.979	1.584	8.339	50.979
4	1.244	6.549	57.528	1.244	6.549	57.528
5	1.166	6.135	63.663	1.166	6.135	63.663
6	1.016	5.346	69.008	1.016	5.346	69.008
7	0.997	5.246	74.254			
8	0.720	3.787	78.041			
9	0.691	3.638	81.679			
10	0.624	3.287	84.965			
11	0.546	2.872	87.837			
12	0.458	2.408	90.245			
13	0.403	2.120	92.365			
14	0.376	1.980	94.344			
15	0.298	1.570	95.915			
16	0.261	1.371	97.286			
17	0.204	1.072	98.358			
18	0.163	0.858	99.215			
19	0.149	0.785	100.000			

Table 5.23 reveals that the scope of variance explained by each factor out of total variance is given as percentage in the third column. It is found that factor 1 account for 30% of variance, factor 2 about 12% of variance, factor 3 about 8% of variance, factor 4& 5 about 6%, factor 6 with 5%, of variance each. The number of factors to be extracted are categorized on the basis of Eigen values being 1 or above for each component. An Eigen value column is the column of sum of squares for the factor which represents the amount of variance in the data. Hence, the model extracts 6 factors for the specified data. The Table 5.24 shows the component matrix for factors.

Table 5.24: Component Matrix for Satisfaction Variables

Statements	Component					
	1	2	3	4	5	6
Providing quick &Speady services	0.726	-0.242	-0.038	0.143	-0.213	0.058
Offering high quality services	0.687	-0.287	-0.063	0.109	-0.187	0.083
Better understanding of customer relatedproblems	0.651	0.333	0.065	0.073	0.122	-0.264
Cost of the product and services	0.635	-0.460	-0.158	-0.066	-0.284	0.058
Safety and security	0.623	-0.396	-0.019	-0.056	-0.139	0.174
Good care by financial services	0.580	-0.374	-0.168	0.066	-0.026	-0.258
Return on deposits	0.563	0.179	-0.165	-0.399	0.153	-0.356
Staff knowledge experience and expertise	0.563	-0.462	-0.202	-0.053	-0.055	-0.054
Banking hours/branch time	0.530	0.066	0.403	-0.423	-0.042	0.187
Staff response	0.517	0.484	-0.059	-0.057	0.264	0.241
Maintaining good hospitality	0.510	-0.125	-0.344	0.173	0.361	0.284
Stationary availability	0.482	0.459	-0.112	0.233	-0.165	0.225
Wide range of product and services	0.483	0.581	-0.124	0.297	-0.357	0.013
Offer fun promotion	0.438	0.563	-0.226	0.089	0.053	0.227
Has friendly and courteous staff	0.378	0.119	0.753	-0.090	-0.322	0.033
Availability and prompt attention of cashier/staff at the counter	0.379	-0.108	0.690	0.341	0.216	0.042
Physical ambience inside the bank	0.549	0.091	0.008	-0.643	0.261	0.150
Adequate parking facilities	0.421	-0.303	0.218	0.355	0.605	-0.029
Utmost care taken while return on deposits	0.587	0.299	0.014	0.078	0.005	-0.636

Extraction Method: Principal Component Analysis

As shown in table 5.24 the Principal Component Analysis has extracted 6 factors which are the co-efficient used to express a standardized variable in terms of the factors. These are termed as factor loadings which shows weight assigned to each factor. Although the factor matrix indicates the relationship between the factors and the individual variables, it is difficult to identify meaningful factors based on this matrix. To identify the factors that significantly summarize the sets of closely related variables, the rotation of the factor matrix is prepared. Varimax rotation is one of the popular methods which is used in the study to simplify the factor structure and extract meaningful factors. The Rotated Factor Matrix using Varimax rotation is highlighted in Table 5.25.

Table 5.25: Rotated Component Matrix of Satisfaction Variables

Statements	Component					
	1	2	3	4	5	6
Quick and Speedy Services	**0.841**	0.029	0.106	0.044	0.067	-0.042
Offering High Quality Services	**0.727**	0.256	0.025	0.128	0.171	0.130
Good Care by Financial Advisor	**0.726**	0.208	0.050	0.084	0.130	0.126
Wide Range of Products and Services	**0.724**	-0.060	0.135	0.136	-0.083	0.096
Brand/ Image of the Bank	**0.723**	0.065	0.189	-0.040	0.142	0.111
Price and Fees of Product and Services	**0.653**	-0.036	0.020	0.345	-0.069	0.154
Return on Deposits	0.124	**0.797**	-0.148	0.278	0.164	-0.159
Safety and Security	0.005	**0.746**	0.215	0.109	-0.075	0.029
Staff Knowledge , Experience and Expertise	0.148	**0.741**	0.015	0.075	0.103	0.001
Staff Response	-0.004	**0.620**	0.441	0.120	0.009	0.209
Better Understanding of customer related problems	0.212	0.115	**0.856**	0.129	0.073	0.028
Is Understanding / Knowing the Customer	0.231	0.124	**0.563**	0.041	0.524	0.034
Inquiry Counter	0.163	0.259	0.023	**0.853**	0.123	0.082
Offer Fun Promotion	0.216	0.131	0.510	**0.596**	-0.067	-0.049
Has Friendly & Courteous Staff	0.163	0.420	0.188	**0.562**	0.157	0.224
Banking Hours / Branch Facilities	0.105	0.103	0.107	0.094	**0.891**	0.032
Good Hospitailty	0.240	-0.041	0.051	0.129	**-0.658**	**0.855**
Adequate Parking Facilities	0.421	-0.303	0.218	0.355	**0.605**	**-0.029**
Physical Appearance	0.109	0.040	-0.057	0.058	**0.578**	**0.665**
My bank is Easily Reachable	0.415	0.335	0.219	-0.069	-0.351	**0.519**

Extraction Method: Principal Component Analysis.

Rotation Method: Varimax with Kaiser Normalization.

It is clear from the Table 5.25 that each factor identifies itself with a few set of variables after 10 iterations. The variables which make out with each of the factors are arranged in descending order and are shown each row and column.

After fixing the common factors, factors score co-efficient is calculated for all variables as each factor is a linear combination of all variables. It is used to estimate factor scores for each individual. The original values of variables are maintained for additional analysis and factor scores are calculated by adding the values of corresponding variables for the particular factor for each respondent. The 19 variables are thus reduced to 6 factors. Details are shown in Table 5.26.

Table 5.26: Statements Relating to Satisfaction Level of the Respondents

Factor Name	Statements
Factor 1 Efficient Services	Quick and Speedy Services
	Offering High Quality of Services
	Good Care by Financial Advisor
	Wide Range of Products and Services
	Brand/ Image of the Bank
	Price and Fees of Product and Services
Factor 2 Basic Services	Return on Deposits
	Safety and Security
	Staff Knowledge , Experience and Expertise
	Staff Response
Factor 3 Performance	Better Understanding of customer related problems
	Is Understanding / Knowing the Customer
Factor 4 Employee Relationship	Inquiry Counter
	Offer Fun Promotion
	Has Friendly & Courteous Staff
Factor 5 Facilities	Banking Hours / Branch Facilities
	Good Hospitality
	Physical Appearance
	Parking Facilities
Factor 6 Bank Layout	Good Hospitality
	Physical Appearance
	My bank is Easily Reachable

Table 5.26 highlights that the Factor 1 is grouped as Efficient Services. It comprises of Quick and Speedy Services, Offering High Quality Services, Good Care by Financial Advisor, Wide Range of Products and Services, Brand/ Image of the Bank and Price & Fees of Product and Services. Factor 2 as Basic Services which includes variable like Return on Deposits, Safety and Security, Staff Knowledge - Experience and Expertise and Staff Response. Factor 3 as Performance, comprise of Understanding of Customer related problems and Is Understanding / Knowing the customer. Factor 4 as Employee Relationship which includes statements like Inquiry Counter, Offer Fun promotion and has friendly & Courteous staff. Factor 5 as Facilities comprises of Banking hours/Branch facilities, Good hospitality, Physical appearance and Parking Facilities. Factor 6 as Bank Layout which comprises of Good hospitality, Physical appearance and My bank is easily Reachable.

Finally, Factor correlation matrix is calculated to find out the correlation between matrix of the factors. It is shown in Table 5.27.

Table 5.27: Component Transformation Matrix

Component	1	2	3	4	5	6
1	0.674	0.444	0.334	0.362	0.206	0.251
2	-0.617	0.701	0.125	0.257	0.090	-0.194
3	-0.236	-0.225	0.016	-0.029	0.888	0.322
4	0.043	0.333	-0.812	-0.032	-0.061	0.472
5	-0.319	-0.121	0.397	0.077	-0.392	0.752
6	0.074	0.367	0.235	-0.892	0.049	0.084

Table 5.27 indicates the factor correlation matrix. If the factors are uncorrelated between themselves, then from the factor correlation matrix, the diagonal elements will be 1 and off diagonal elements will be 0. Since, matrix has been rotated with Varimax, barring various variables all other variables are found to contain, even if not zero correlation but fairly low correlation.

5.6. Satisfaction Level of the Respondents about the Brand Management in Commercial Banks: Multiple Regression Analysis

Multiple Regression Analysis has been applied to examine the strength of relationship between all the independent variables of the sample respondents and the dependent variables such as gender, age, educational qualification, marital status, occupation, annual income and total experience. In this chapter, seven regression equation models is worked out to ascertain the influence of different sets of independent variables on satisfaction. The regression is estimated using cross-section data of 384 private sector and 196 public sector banks sample customer.

Public Sector Banks

Regression Model I: $Y = f(X_1)$

Bivariate regression analysis provided information to test the following hypothesis.

H_o: There is no relationship between satisfaction (Y) and age of customers (X_1).

Table 5.28 shows the results of estimated regression equation of Y on X_1. The regression equation is Y 19.696+0.355 X_1

Regression Equation reveals that only 0.10% of the total variation in variable Y was explained by variable X_1 ($R^2 = 0.010$). 'F' statistic was calculated to test the significance of R^2. As calculated value of 'F' was greater than the table value, R^2 was significantly greater from zero. It implies that the estimated regression model was significant. Hence, the hypothesis was rejected and it was concluded that there is a relationship between satisfaction and age of respondents.

Table 5.28: Results of Regression Equation of Y on X_1

Variables	Unstandardised Coefficients B	Std. Error	Standardised Coefficients Beta	't' statistic
Constant	19.696	0.368		53.595
Gender	0.355	0.247	0.102	1.434
R			0.102	
R^2			0.010	
$\overline{R}^2$			0.005	
			2.056	
'F'				

The 't' statistics reveals the Beta coefficient 0.102 of variable X_1 was significant at 1% level indicates that the coefficient of age was positively associated with satisfaction. The rate of increase that could be achieved was 0.102 for every unit change in age. It means that when age of the customers increases by one year, their satisfaction score increases by 0.102. Hence increasing number of independent variable provides better regression line.

Regression Model II: Y = f(X1 and X_2)

Regression equation (Model II) was developed by increasing the number of independent variables to two. Multiple regression analysis provides information to test the following hypothesis.

H_0: There is no relationship between satisfaction (Y) and independent variables X_1 and X_2.

Table 5.29 shows the results of estimated regression equation of Y on X_1 and X_2. The regression equation was Y= 19.585+0.375 X_1+0.078 X_2.

Table 5.29: Results of Regression Equation of Y on X_1 and X_2

Variables	Unstandardised Coefficients B	Std. Error	Standardised Coefficients Beta	't' statistic
Constant	19.585	0.442		44.287
Gender	0.375	0.252	0.108	1.490
Age	0.078	0.173	0.033	0.453
R			0.107	
R^2			0.012	
$\overline{R}^2$			0.001	
'F'			1.127	

Multiple Regression Analysis has revealed that the group of two independent variables influence the dependent variable to the extent of 1.2 per cent (R^2= 0.012).The computed value of 'F' (1.127) was larger than the tabulated value of 'F' (4.61) at 1% level of significance for 2 & 193 degrees of freedom (K and n-k-1 d.f). The regression model was quite effective, there was linear relationship between independent variables, and dependent variable i.e. 'F' was significant. Hence, the hypothesis was rejected and it was concluded that there is a relationship between independent variables and dependent variable.

It is necessary to find whether the additional variable gives more meaningful regression equation. Both R^2 and adjusted R^2 increased by adding the variable X_2. The regression equation is not better than the previous one if adjusted R^2 decreases when a variable is added.

The 't' statistics reveals the Beta coefficient 0.412 of variable X_1 and 0.319 of variable X_2 was significant at 1% level. It indicates that the coefficients of two independent variables were positively associated with satisfaction.

The rate of increase that could be achieved with variable Y is 0.108 for every unit change in variable X_1 and 0.033 for every unit change in variable X_2.

REGRESSION MODEL III: $Y = f(X_1, X2, \text{ and } X_3)$

Regression equation (Model III) was developed by increasing the number of independent variables to three. Multiple regression analysis provides information to test the following hypothesis.

H_o: There is no relationship between satisfaction (Y) and independent variables X_1, X_2 and X_3.

Table 5.30 shows the results of estimated regression equation of Y on X_1, X_2 and X_3.

The regression equation was $Y = 64.524+1.551X_1+1.977X_2+30.457X_3$

Table 5.30 shows that the Multiple Regression equation was found statistically a good fit as R^2 is 0.458. It shows that the three independent variables contribute about 45.8% of variation in dependent variable and 'F' statistics shows that this was statistically significant at 1% level. Hence, the hypothesis was rejected and therefore it can be concluded that the satisfaction of customers depends on variables X_1, X_2 and X_3.

Table 5.30: Results of Regression Equation of Y on X_1, X_2 and X_3

Variables	Unstandardised Coefficients B	Std. Error	Standardised Coefficients Beta	't' statistic
Constant	20.061	0.510		39.317
Gender	0.320	0.252	0.092	1.269
Age	0.144	0.175	0.061	0.824
Educational Qualification	0.256	0.139	0.135	1.835
'R'			0.169	
'R²'			0.029	
$\overline{R}^2$			0.013	
'F'			1.883	

All the three independent variables were positively associated with dependent variable. The 't' statistic reveals that the coefficients of all the three variables were statistically significant, implying their relationship was stronger with satisfaction.

The rate of increase that could be achieved with variable Y is 0.526 for every unit change in variable X_1; 0.304 for every unit change in variable X_2 and 0.288 for X_3.

REGRESSION MODEL IV: $Y = \int(X_1, X_2, X_3 \text{ and } X_4)$

Regression equation (Model IV) was developed by increasing the number of independent variables to four. Multiple regression analysis provides information to test the following hypothesis.

H_o: There is no relationship between satisfaction (Y) and independent variables X_1, X_2, X_3 and X_4

Table 5.31 shows the results of estimated regression equation of Y on X_1, X_2, X_3 and X_4.The regression equation was

$$Y = 18.586 + 0.334\,X_1 + 0.524\,X_2 + 0.328\,X_3 + 0.741\,X_4.$$

Table 5.31: Results of Regression Equation of Y on X_1, X_2, X_3 and X_4

Variables	Unstandardised Coefficients B	Std. Error	Standardised Coefficients Beta	't' statistic
Constant	18.586	0.899		20.679
Gender	0.334	0.250	0.096	1.334
Age	0.524	0.258	0.221	2.027
Educational Qualification	0.328	0.143	0.174	2.297
Marital Status	0.741	0.373	0.209	1.986
'R'			0.220	
'R²'			0.048	
$\overline{R}^2$			0.028	
'F'			2.419	

The Multiple Regression equation was found statistically a good fit as $R^2$is 4.8. It shows that the four independent variables contribute about 0.48% of variation in dependent variable and 'F' statistics shows this was statistically significant at 1% level. Hence, the hypothesis was rejected and therefore it can be concluded that the satisfaction of customers depends on variables X_1, X_2, X_3 and X_4.

All the four independent variables were positively associated with dependent variable. The 't' statistic reveals that the coefficients of all the four variables were statistically significant, implying their relationship was stronger with satisfaction.

The rate of increase that could be achieved with variable Y is 0.096 for every unit change in variable X_1; 0.221 for every unit change in variable X_2; 0.174 for every unit change in X_3 and 0.209 for every unit change in variable X_4.

REGRESSION MODEL V: $Y = f(X_1, X_2, X_3, X_4$ and $X_5)$

Regression equation (Model V) was developed by increasing the number of independent variables to five. Multiple regression analysis provides information to test the following hypothesis. Multiple regression analysis provided information to test the below hypothesis.

H_o : There is no relationship between satisfaction (Y) and independent variables X_1 , X_2 , ... X_5.

Table 5.32 shows the results of estimated regression equation of Y on X_1, X_2, ... X_5. The regression equation was

$$Y = 18.574 + 0.331X_1 + 0.511X_2 + 0.333X_3 + 0.733X_4 + 0.024X_5.$$

Table 5.32 shows that the Multiple Regression equation was found statistically a good fit as R^2 is 4.8. It shows that the five independent variables contribute about 0.48% of variation in dependent variable and 'F' statistics shows that this was statistically significant at 1% level. Hence, the hypothesis was rejected and therefore it can be concluded that the satisfaction of customers depends on variables X_1, X_2, X_3, X_4 and X_5.

Table 5.32: Results of Regression Equation of Y on X_1, X_2, ... X_5

Variables	Unstandardised Coefficients B	Std. Error	Standardised Coefficients Beta	't' statistic
Constant	18.574	0.903		20.575
Gender	0.331	0.251	0.096	1.318
Age	0.511	0.267	0.215	1.915
Educational Qualification	0.333	0.145	0.176	2.298
Marital Status	0.733	0.376	0.207	1.947
Occupation	0.024	0.110	0.016	0.216
'R'			0.220	
'R²'			0.048	
$\overline{R}^2$			0.023	
			1.935	
'F'				

All the five independent variables were positively associated with dependent variable. The 't' statistic reveals that the coefficients of all the five variables were statistically significant, implying their relationship was stronger with satisfaction.

The rate of increase that could be achieved with variable Y is 0.096 for every unit change in variable X_1; 0.215 for every unit change in variable X_2; 0.176 for every unit change in X_3; 0.207 for every unit change in X_4 and 0.016 for every unit change in variable X_5.

REGRESSION MODEL VI: Y =f(X1, X_2,X_3,X_4 ,$X_5$and X_6)

Regression equation (Model VI) was developed by increasing the number of independent variables to six. Multiple regression analysis provides information to test the following hypothesis.

H_o : There is no relationship between satisfaction (Y) and independent variablesX_1 , X_2, ... X_6.

Table 5.33 shows the results of estimated regression equation of Y on X_1, X_2, ... X_6 .

The regression equation was

$$Y = 19.173 + 0.320X_1 + 0.454X_2 + 0.352X_3 + 0.717X_4 + 0.023X_5 + 0.270X_6.$$

Table 5.33: Results of Regression Equation of Y on X_1, X_2, ...X_6

Variables	Unstandardised Coefficients B	Std. Error	Standardised Coefficients Beta	't' statistic
Constant	19.173	0.987		19.430
Gender	0.320	0.251	0.093	1.278
Age	0.454	0.269	0.191	1.690
Educational Qualification	0.352	0.145	0.186	2.425
Marital Status	0.717	0.375	0.202	1.911
Occupation	0.023	0.109	0.016	0.214
Annual Income	0.270	0.183	0.107	1.478
'R'			0.244	
'R²'			0.059	
$\overline{R}^2$			0.029	
'F'			1.987	

The Multiple Regression equation was found statistically a good fit as R^2 is 5.9. It shows that the six independent variables contribute about 0.59% of variation in dependent variable and 'F' statistics shows that this was statistically significant at 1% level. Hence, the hypothesis was rejected and therefore it can be concluded that the satisfaction of customers depends on variables X_1, X_2,X_3,X_4 ,$X_5$and X_6.

All the five independent variables were positively associated with dependent variable. The 't' statistic reveals that the coefficients of all the six variables were statistically significant, implying their relationship was stronger with satisfaction.

The rate of increase that could be achieved with variable Y is 0.093 for every unit change in variable X_1; 0.191 for every unit change in variable X_2; 0.186 for every unit change in X_3; 0.202for every unit change in X_4 , 0.016 for every unit change in X_5 and 0.107 for every unit change in X_6.

REGRESSION MODEL VII: Y = f(X$_1$, X$_2$, X$_3$, X$_4$, X5, X6and X$_7$)

Regression equation (Model VII) was developed by increasing the number of independent variables to seven. Multiple regression analysis provides information to test the following hypothesis.

H_o : There is no relationship between satisfaction (Y) and independent variablesX_1 , X_2, ... X_7.

Table 5.34 shows the results of estimated regression equation of Y on X_1, X_2, ... X_7. The regression equation was

$$Y = 19.711+0.413X_1+0.572X_2+0.356X_3+0.778X_4++ 0.029X_5 + 0.280X_6 + 0.179X_7.$$

Regression Equation reveals that 0.73% of the total variation in variable Y was explained by seven independent variables (R^2 = 0.073). 'F' statistic was calculated to test the significance of R^2. As calculated value of 'F' was greater than the table value, R^2 was significantly greater from zero. It implies that the estimated regression model was significant. Hence, the hypothesis was rejected and it was concluded that there is a relationship between the dependent variable and seven independent variables.

Table 5.34 reveals that all the seven independent variables were positively associated with dependent variable. The 't' statistic reveals that the coefficients of all the seven variables were statistically significant, implying their relationship was stronger with satisfaction.

Table 5.34: Results of Regression Equation of Y on X_1, X_2, ... X_7

Variables	Unstandardised Coefficients B	Std. Error	Standardised Coefficients Beta	't' statistic
Constant	19.711	1.035		19.052
Gender	0.413	0.256	0.119	01.614
Age	0.572	0.277	0.241	2.067
Educational Qualification	0.356	0.144	0.188	2.468
Marital Status	0.778	0.375	0.220	2.073
Occupation	0.029	0.109	0.020	0.270
Annual Income	0.280	0.182	0.111	1.541
Total Experience with this Bank	0.179	0.108	0.125	1.656
'R'	0.270			
'R²'	0.073			
$\overline{R}^2$	0.038			
'F'	2.111			

The rate of increase that could be achieved with variable Y is 0.119 for every unit change in variable X_1; 0.241 for every unit change in variable X_2; 0.188 for every unit change in X_3; 0.220 for every unit change in X_4; 0.020 for every unit change in X_5; 0.111for every unit change in X_6 and 0.125 for every unit change in X_7.

Interpretation of Regression Coefficient when Regressor is a Binary Variable (Dummy Variable)

In the above analysis, X_2, X_3, X_5, X_6 and X_7 were continuous variables; X_1, and X_4 were binary regressors. The mechanics of regression with a binary regressor were the same as if it is continuous. The interpretation of coefficient, however is different.

In the Regression Equation VII, the estimated coefficient of gender (X_1) is positive and statistically significant. According to the estimate, the effect of an male customer in the satisfaction score has an increase of (0.241 multiplied by 1) 0.241, whereas the effect of a female customer in the satisfaction score is (0.241 multiplied by 0) nil. As X_1 is not continuous, it is not useful to think of its coefficient as a slope; indeed, because X_3 can take on only two values, $X_1 = 1$, if the respondent's gender is male and $X_1 = 0$, if the respondent's gender is female. The satisfaction score of male customers will be more, on average, by 0.241 than female customers.

Similarly, the difference in satisfaction score of marital status (X_4) is 0.220.The satisfaction score of married customers will be more, on average, by 0.052 than unmarried customers.

5.7.　A Summary of Regression Model of Independent Variables on Total Satisfaction (Public Sector)

The results of seven regression equations were summarised in table 5.35. The multiple regression models for customers satisfaction reveals that the model fit increases from 0.102 to 0.270 by adding more variables such as gender, age, educational qualification, marital status, occupation, annual income and total experience with this bank to the independent variable in a step-by-step process.

The mean score of this dimension is 60.10. The adjusted R square also shows an increase from 0.005 to 0.038. This indicates that the increase of eight independent variables is significant in the regression equation.

Table 5.35: Analysis of Regression of Independent Variables on Satisfaction Score

Dependent Variable: Total Satisfaction							
Regressor	Regression Model						
	I	II	III	IV	V	VI	VII
Gender	0.102	0.108	0.092	0.096	0.096	0.093	0.119
Age		0.033	0.061	0.221	0.215	0.191	0.241
Educational Qualification			0.135	0.174	0.176	0.186	0.188
Marital Status				0.209	0.207	0.202	0.220
Occupation					0.016	0.016	0.020
Annual Income						0.107	0.111
Total Experience with this Bank							0.125
Summary Statistics and Join Tests							
SER	0.368	0.442	0.510	0.899	0.903	0.987	1.035
R	0.102	0.107	0.169	0.220	0.220	0.244	0.270
R^2	**0.010**	**0.012**	**0.029**	**0.048**	**0.048**	**0.059**	**0.073**
Adjusted R^2	0.005	0.001	0.013	0.028	0.023	0.029	0.038
N	196	196	196	196	196	196	196

Private Sector Banks

REGRESSION MODEL I: $Y = f(X_1)$

Bivariate regression analysis provided information to test the following hypothesis.

H_0: There is no relationship between satisfaction (Y) and age of customers (X_1).

Table 5.36 shows the results of estimated regression equation of Y on X_1. The regression equation is $Y = 17.479 + 1.098X_1$

Regression Equation reveals that only 0.69% of the total variation in variable Y was explained by variable X_1 ($R^2 = 0.069$). 'F' statistic was calculated to test the significance of R^2. As calculated value of 'F' was greater than the table value, R^2 was significantly greater from zero. It implies that the estimated regression model was significant. Hence, the hypothesis was rejected and it was concluded that there is a relationship between satisfaction and age of respondents.

Table: 5.36: Results of Regression Equation of Y on X_1

Variables	Unstandardised Coefficients B	Std. Error	Standardised Coefficients Beta	't' statistic
Constant	17.479	0.308		56.763
Gender	1.098	0.206	0.263	5.321
R			0.263	
R^2			0.069	
$\overline{R}^2$			0.067	
'F'			28.313	

The 't' statistics reveals the Beta coefficient 0.263 of variable X_1 was significant at 1% level indicates that the coefficient of age was positively associated with satisfaction. The rate of increase that could be achieved was 0.263 for every unit change in age. It means that when age of the customers increases by one year, their satisfaction score increases by 0.263. Hence, increasing number of independent variable provides better regression line.

REGRESSION MODEL II: $Y = \int(X1 \text{ and } X_2)$

Regression equation (Model II) was developed by increasing the number of independent variables to two. Multiple regression analysis provides information to test the following hypothesis.

H_0: There is no relationship between satisfaction (Y) and independent variables X_1 and X_2.

Table 5.37 shows the results of estimated regression equation of Y on X_1 and X_2. The regression equation was $Y=17.167 +1.112X_1+0.158X_2$.

Table 5.37: Results of Regression Equation of Y on X_1 and X_2

Variables	Unstandardised Coefficients B	Std. Error	Standardised Coefficients Beta	't' statistic
Constant	17.167	0.463		37.060
Gender	1.112	0.207	0.266	5.372
Age	0.158	0.175	0.045	0.901
R			0.266	
R^2			0.071	
$\overline{R}^2$			0.066	
'F'			14.555	

Multiple Regression Analysis has revealed that the group of two independent variables influence the dependent variable to the extent of 7.1 per cent (R^2=7.1). The computed value of 'F' (14.555) was larger than the tabulated value of 'F' (4.61) at 1% level of significance for 2 & 381 degrees of freedom (K and n-k-1 d.f). The regression model was quite effective, there was linear relationship between independent variables, and dependent variable i.e. 'F' was significant. Hence, the hypothesis was rejected and it was concluded that there is a relationship between independent variables and dependent variable.

It is necessary to find whether the additional variable gives more meaningful regression equation. Both R^2 and adjusted R^2 increased by adding the variable X_2. The regression equation is not better than the previous one if adjusted R^2 decreases when a variable is added. The 't' statistics reveals the Beta coefficient 0.266 of variable X_1 and 0.045 of variable X_2 was significant at 1% level. It indicates that the coefficients of two independent variables were positively associated with satisfaction.

The rate of increase that could be achieved with variable Y is 0.266 for every unit change in variable X_1 and 0.045 for every unit change in variable X_2.

REGRESSION MODEL III: Y = ∫ (X₁, X2, and X₃)

Regression equation (Model III) was developed by increasing the number of independent variables to three. Multiple regression analysis provides information to test the following hypothesis.

H_o: There is no relationship between satisfaction (Y) and independent variables X_1, X_2 and X_3.

Table 5.11 shows the results of estimated regression equation of Y on X_1, X_2 and X_3.

The regression equation was Y =18.280 +1.131X_1+0.203X_2+0.455X_3

Table 5.38shows that the Multiple Regression equation was found statistically a good fit as R^2 is 0.112. It shows that the three independent variables contribute about 11.2% of variation in dependent variable and 'F' statistics shows that this was statistically significant at 1% level. Hence, the hypothesis was rejected and therefore it can be concluded that the satisfaction of customers depends on variables X_1, X_2 and X_3.

Table 5.38: Results of Regression Equation of Y on X_1,X_2 and X_3

Variables	Unstandardised Coefficients B	Std. Error	Standardised Coefficients Beta	't' Statistic
(Constant)	18.280	0.526		34.749
Gender	1.131	0.203	0.271	5.578
Age	0.203	0.172	0.057	1.180
Educational Qualification	-0.455	0.109	0.202	4.176
R			0.334	
R^2			0.112	
$\overline{R}^2$			0.105	
'F'			15.935	

All the three independent variables were positively associated with dependent variable. The 't' statistic reveals that the coefficients of all the three variables were statistically significant, implying their relationship was stronger with satisfaction. The rate of increase that could be achieved with variable Y is 0.271for every unit change in variable X_1; 0.057 for every unit change in variable X_2 and 0.202 for X_3.

REGRESSION MODEL IV: Y = ∫(X₁, X₂, X₃ and X₄)

Regression equation (Model IV) was developed by increasing the number of independent variables to four. Multiple regression analysis provides information to test the following hypothesis.

H_o: There is no relationship between satisfaction (Y) and independent variablesX_1, X_2, X_3 and X_4

Table 5.39 shows the results of estimated regression equation of Y on X_1, X_2, X_3 and X_4.The regression equation was

$$Y = 18.270+1.130X_1+0.205X_2+0.455X_3+0.006X_4.$$

Table 5.39: Results of Regression Equation of Y on X_1, X_2,X_3 and X_4

Variables	Unstandardised Coefficients B	Std. Error	Standardised Coefficients Beta	't' statistic
(Constant)	18.270	0.761		24.013
Gender	1.130	0.206	0.270	5.474
Age	0.205	0.218	0.058	0.940
Educational Qualification	0.455	0.109	0.202	4.165
Marital Status	0.006	0.291	0.001	0.019
'R'			0.334	
'R²'			0.112	
$\overline{R}^2$			0.102	
'F'			11.920	

The Multiple Regression equation was found statistically a good fit as R^2 is 11.2. It shows that the four independent variables contribute about 11.2% of variation in dependent variable and 'F' statistics shows this was statistically significant at 1% level. Hence, the hypothesis was rejected and therefore it can be concluded that the satisfaction of customers depends on variables X_1, X_2, X_3 and X_4.

All the four independent variables were positively associated with dependent variable. The 't' statistic reveals that the coefficients of all the four variables were statistically significant, implying their relationship was stronger with satisfaction.

The rate of increase that could be achieved with variable Y is 0.270for every unit change in variable X_1; 0.058for every unit change in variable X_2; 0.202for every unit change in X_3 and 0.001for every unit change in variable X_4.

REGRESSION MODEL V: Y = ƒ(X1, X_2, $X_{3,x4}$ and X_5)

Regression equation (Model V) was developed by increasing the number of independent variables to five. Multiple regression analysis provides information to test the following hypothesis. Multiple regression analysis provided information to test the below hypothesis.

H_o : There is no relationship between satisfaction (Y) and independent variablesX_1, X_2, ... X_5.

Table 5.40 shows the results of estimated regression equation of Y on X_1, X_2, ... X_5. The regression equation was

$$Y = 17.811+1.222X_1+0.018X_2+0.475X_3+0.143X_4+0.363X_5.$$

Table 5.13 shows that the Multiple Regression equation was found statistically a good fit as R^2 is 0.143. It shows that the five independent variables contribute about 14.3% of variation in dependent variable and 'F' statistics shows that this was statistically significant at 1% level. Hence, the hypothesis was rejected and therefore it can be concluded that the satisfaction of customers depends on variables X_1, X_2, X_3, X_4 and X_5.

Table 5.40: Results of Regression Equation of Y on X_1, X_2, ... X_5

Variables	Unstandardised Coefficients B	Std. Error	Standardised Coefficients Beta	't' statistic
Constant	17.811	0.759		23.474
Gender	1.222	0.205	0.292	5.972
Age	0.018	0.221	0.005	0.082
Educational Qualification	0.475	0.108	0.211	4.411
Marital Status	0.143	0.289	0.031	0.497
Occupation	0.363	0.098	0.182	3.691
'R'	0.378			
'R²'	0.143			
$\overline{R}^2$	0.131			
'F'	12.578			

All the five independent variables were positively associated with dependent variable. The 't' statistic reveals that the coefficients of all the five variables were statistically significant, implying their relationship was stronger with satisfaction.

The rate of increase that could be achieved with variable Y is 0.292for every unit change in variable X_1; 0.005 for every unit change in variable X_2; 0.211for every unit change in X_3; 0.031for every unit change in X_4 and 0.182for every unit change in variable X_5.

REGRESSION MODEL VI: Y =f(X1, X_2,X_3,X_4 ,$X_5$and X_6)

Regression equation (Model VI) was developed by increasing the number of independent variables to six. Multiple regression analysis provides information to test the following hypothesis.

H_0 : There is no relationship between satisfaction (Y) and independent variablesX_1 , X_2, ... X_6.

Table 5.41 shows the results of estimated regression equation of Y on X_1, X_2, ... X_6 .

The regression equation was

$$Y = 17.360+1.184X_1+0.060X_2+0.505X_3+0.240X_4+0.337X_5+ 0.574X_6.$$

Table 5.41: Results of Regression Equation of Y on X_1, X_2, ...X_6

Variables	Unstandardised Coefficients B	Std. Error	Standardised Coefficients Beta	't' statistic
Constant	17.360	0.753		23.039
Gender	1.184	0.201	0.283	5.888
Age	0.060	0.218	0.017	0.277
Educational Qualification	0.505	0.106	0.224	4.765
Marital Status	0.240	0.284	0.052	0.845
Occupation	0.337	0.097	0.169	3.486
Annual Income	0.574	0.146	0.186	3.924
'R'			0.420	
'R²'			0.176	
$\overline{R}^2$			0.163	
'F'			13.448	

The Multiple Regression equation was found statistically a good fit as R^2 is 17.6. It shows that the six independent variables contribute about 17.6% of variation in dependent variable and 'F' statistics shows that this was statistically significant at 1% level. Hence, the hypothesis was rejected and therefore it can be concluded that the satisfaction of customers depends on variables X_1, X_2, X_3, X_4, X_5 and X_6.

All the five independent variables were positively associated with dependent variable. The 't' statistic reveals that the coefficients of all the six variables were statistically significant, implying their relationship was stronger with satisfaction.

The rate of increase that could be achieved with variable Y is 0.283for every unit change in variable X_1; 0.017for every unit change in variable X_2; 0.224for every unit change in X_3; 0.052for every unit change in X_4 , 0.169for every unit change in X_5 and 0.186 for every unit change in X_6.

REGRESSION MODEL VII: Y = f(X_1, X_2, X_3, X_4, X5, X6and X_7)

Regression equation (Model VII) was developed by increasing the number of independent variables to seven. Multiple regression analysis provides information to test the following hypothesis.

H_0 : There is no relationship between satisfaction (Y) and independent variablesX_1 , X_2, ... X_7.

Table 5.42shows the results of estimated regression equation of Y on X_1, X_2, ... X_7. The regression equation was

$$Y = 17.242+1.189X_1+0.048X_2+0.505X_3+0.242X_4+0.339X_5+ 0.571X_6 + 0.029X_7.$$

Regression Equation reveals that 18% of the total variation in variable Y was explained by seven independent variables (R^2 = 0.177). 'F' statistic was calculated to test the significance of R^2. As calculated value of 'F' was greater than the table value, R^2 was significantly greater from zero. It implies that the estimated regression model was significant. Hence, the hypothesis was rejected and it was concluded that there is a relationship between the dependent variable and seven independent variables.

Table 5.42 reveals that all the seven independent variables were positively associated with dependent variable. The 't' statistic reveals that the coefficients of all the seven variables were statistically significant, implying their relationship was stronger with satisfaction.

Table 5.42: Results of Regression Equation of Y on X_1, X_2, ... X_7

Variables	Unstandardised Coefficients B	Std. Error	Standardised Coefficients Beta	't' statistic
Constant	17.242	0.806		21.401
Gender(female=0) (male=1)	1.189	0.202	0.285	5.896
Age	0.048	0.220	0.014	0.217
Educational Qualification	0.505	0.106	0.225	4.763
Marital Status(unmarried=0) (married=1)	0.242	0.285	0.052	0.849
Occupation	0.339	0.097	0.170	3.499
Annual income	0.571	0.147	0.185	3.896
Total Experience with this Bank	0.029	0.069	0.020	0.416
'R'	0.420			
'R²'	0.177			
$\overline{R}^2$	0.161			
'F'	11.526			

The rate of increase that could be achieved with variable Y is 0.285for every unit change in variable X_1; 0.014for every unit change in variable X_2; 0.225for every unit change in X_3; 0.052for every unit change in X_4; 0.170 for every unit change in X_5; 0.185for every unit change in X_6 and 0.020 for every unit change in X_7.

Interpretation of Regression Coefficient when Regressor is a Binary Variable (Dummy Variable)

In the above analysis X_2, X_3, X_5, $X_6$and X_7 were continuous variables; X_1 and X_4 was binary regressors. The mechanics of regression with a binary regressor are the same as if it is continuous. The interpretation of coefficient, however is different. In the Regression Equation VII, the estimated coefficient of gender(X_1) is positive and statistically significant. According to the estimate, the effect of an male customer in the satisfaction score has an increase of (0.014

multiplied by 1) 0.014, whereas the effect of a female customer in the satisfaction score was (0.014 multiplied by 0) nil. As X_1 is not continuous, it is not useful to think of its coefficient as a slope; indeed, because X_1 can take on only two values, $X_1 = 1$, if the respondent's gender is male and $X_1 = 0$, if the respondent's gender is female. The satisfaction score of male customers will be more, on average, by 0.041 than female customers.

Similarly, the difference in satisfaction score of marital status (X_4) is 0.052.The satisfaction score of married customers will be more, on average, by 0.052 than unmarried customers.

5.8. A Summary of Regression Model of Independent Variables on Total Satisfaction (Private Sector)

The results of seven regression equations were summarised in table 5.43. The multiple regression models for customers satisfaction reveals that the model fit increases from 0.263 to 0.420 by adding more variables such as gender, age, educational qualification, marital status, occupation, annual income and total experience with this bank to the independent variable in a step-by-step process. The mean score of this dimension is60.49. The adjusted R square also shows an increase from 0.067 to 0.161. This indicates that the increase of eight independent variables was significant in the regression equation.

Table 5.43: Analysis of Regression of Independent Variables on Satisfaction Score

Dependent Variable: Total Satisfaction							
Regressor	**Regression Model**						
	I	II	III	IV	V	VI	VII
Gender	0.263	0.266	0.271	0.270	0.292	0.283	0.285
Age		0.045	0.057	0.058	0.005	0.017	0.014
Educational Qualification			0.202	0.202	0.211	0.224	0.225
Marital Status				0.001	0.031	0.052	0.052
Occupation					0.182	0.169	0.170
Annual Income						0.186	0.185
Total Experience with this Bank							0.020
Summary Statistics and Join Tests							
SER	0.308	0.463	0.526	0.761	0.759	0.753	0.806
R	0.263	0.266	0.334	0.334	0.378	0.420	0.420
R^2	**0.069**	**0.071**	**0.112**	**0.112**	**0.143**	**0.176**	**0.177**
Adjusted R^2	0.067	0.066	0.105	0.102	0.131	0.163	0.161
N	384	384	384	384	384	384	384

5.9.   Summary

In this chapter, satisfaction of the sample customer towards brand management in commercial bank, necessary primary data are gathered using questionnaires. For which, 19 relevant statements have been prearranged in the questionnaires by using Rensis Likert's 5 point rating scale technique. Such collected data have been calculated with the help of various statistical tools like Chi-square test, 'F' test, 'Z' test, Contingency Co-efficient at 1% level of significance and Cronbach's Alpha Reliability Analysis. The satisfaction statements comprised and arranged into a meaningful set using Factor Analysis. Further, Multiple Regression Analysis has been applied to analyses the influence of various independent variables over satisfaction of the sample customers towards brand management in commercial banks.

Level of Satisfaction

It is found that in private sector bank majority (54.8%) of the sample customers are having low level satisfaction among selected commercial bank customers towards brand management. The mean score is 56.7 and standard deviation is 8.56.

It is found that in public sector bank majority (29.0%) of the sample customers are having low level satisfaction among selected commercial bank customers towards brand management. The mean score is 56.80 and standard deviation is 8.45.

Age and Satisfaction Level

In age-wise analysis, it is found that in private and public sector banks respondents who are at the age of above 50 years category low level satisfaction compared to other age groups.

Gender and Satisfaction Level

In gender-wise analysis, it is found that in private and public sector banks male customers are low satisfaction than the female customers.

Marital Status and Satisfaction Level

While considering the marital status, in the case of private sector sample customers found that 84.4% of the unmarried sample customers and 82.2% of the married sample customers are having low satisfaction. In the case of public sector banks, it is found that 87% of the unmarried and 84.8% married sample customers and are having low level satisfaction about their brand management in banks.

Educational Level and Satisfaction Level

Regarding the educational level, it is found that in both private and public sector banks, the sample respondents belonging to PG and above have low satisfaction followed by other groups.

Occupational Status and Satisfaction Level

While examine the occupational status, it is evident that in the case of private sector 92.1% of the Student/Housewife have low satisfactory rates followed other sample customers while in case of public sector 92.3% of the pensioner have low satisfactory rates compared to other sample customers.

Annual Income and Satisfaction Level

In the aspect of annual income, it is found that in the case of private sector & public sector banks above 5, 00,000 income sample customers are having low level Satisfaction.

From the inferences of the results of Chi-square test, it is found that there is no significant association between the independent variables (age, gender, educational qualification, marital status, occupation and annual income) of the sample towards brand management in commercial banks.

In 'F' test analysis; it is found that the association between various socio-economic characteristics like age, educational qualification, occupational status and annual income of the sample customer and their mean satisfaction level is found to be insignificant.

From 'Z' test analysis, it can be concluded that there is no significant difference in the mean scores of gender and marital status and satisfaction level of selected commercial bank customers towards brand management.

From the Cronbach's Alpha reliability test, it is noted that the factors used to examine the satisfaction level of the sample respondents about the banks are reliable and have an acceptable point of internal consistency.

Principal component analysis was used since the objective is to summarize most of the original information in a minimum number of factors for prediction purpose.

Varimax rotations were used in the study to simplify the factor structure by maximizing the variance of a column of pattern matrix. An Eigen value is the column sum of squares for a factor represents the amount of variance in data. After determination of the common factors, factors scores were estimated for each factor. The common factor themselves were expressed as linear combinations of the observed variables.

In Factor Analysis, 19 statements used to test the satisfaction level of the sample towards brand management in commercial banks have been grouped into 6 factors viz., efficient services, basic services, performance, employee relationship, facilities and bank layout.

Regression analysis is used to examine the relationship between satisfaction score of the customers and independent variables such as gender, age, educational qualification, marital status, occupation, annual income and total experience with this bank.

In this chapter, seven separate regression equation models were worked out to ascertain the influence of different set of independent variables on satisfaction.

The regressions were estimated using cross-section data of 384 private sector and 196 public sector bank sample customers. The results of a regression model were testedto examine its significance include the R^2; the model F statistic; the individual regression coefficients for each independent variable; their associate 't' statistics; and the individual beta coefficients.

In the case of public sector bank Regression Equation reveals that 7.3% of the total variation in variable Y was explained by seven independent variables (R^2 = 0.073). In the case of private sector bank Regression Equation reveals that 17.7% of the total variation in variable Y was explained by seven independent variables (R^2 = 0.177).'F' statistic was calculated to test the significance of R^2. As calculated value of 'F' is greater than the table value, R^2 was significantly greater from zero. It implies that the estimated regression model was significant. Hence, it was concluded that there is a significant relationship between the dependent variable and seven independent variables.

All the seven independent variables were positively associated with dependent variable in low level of satisfaction. The 't' statistic reveals that the coefficients of all the seven variables were statistically significant, implying their relationship was less satisfaction.

CHAPTER VI

A SUMMARY OF FINDINGS, SUGGESTIONS AND CONCLUSION

6.1. Introduction

A banking institution is indispensable in a modern society. Banking system which constitutes the core of the financial sector plays a critical role in transmitting monitory policy impulses to the entire economic development. The importance of commercial banks in the process of economic development has been recognized by all. The commercial banks play an important role in all economies. Banking is a service industry and multi-dimensional in nature.

"Now-a-days banks become part and parcel of our life and without banks can't survive and sustain. Every customer has a particular level of expectation regarding services that he gets from his bank".

Brand is important role in success of banking sectors. Brand success depends on financial organization capability to fulfill its promises. A successful brand name contains the following features

- Distinctiveness-it is identified at once and differentiated from the competition.
- Relevance-envisages service benefits.
- Significance-easy to recognize, remember and pronounce.
- Flexibility - convenient for new financial products and services introduction into the financial organisation offer.

This study was conducted to assess the Level of Perception, Attitude and Satisfaction in commercial banking sectors. This chapter summarizes the findings and conclusions of the study and offer suggestions for enhancing the perception level of customers in brand management of commercial banking sectors.

6.2. Objectives of the Study

The objectives of the study are as follows:

1. An overview of progress and development of brand management in commercial banks.
2. To study the customers' perception towards brand management in selected commercial banks.
3. To study the customers' attitude for brand management in selected commercial banks.
4. To measure the level of customer satisfaction among selected commercial bank customers towards brand management.

6.3.   Hypotheses

On the basis of the framed objectives, discussions with the field experts and on the basis of the review of various relevant studies, various null hypotheses have been framed and the same have been tested with various statistical tools.

6.4.   Data Collection

The study is based on both primary and secondary data. The primary data were collected from the respondents by using well structured questionnaires. The validity of any research is based on the systematic method of data collection and analysis. The required primary data were collected from 580 sample respondents.

6.5.   Sampling Scheme

Erode district occupies an important position both in industrial and agricultural aspects. Hence, for the present study Erode district has been purposively selected. There are 36 Commercial Banks functioning in Erode District as on March 2014. 21 are Public Sector banks and 15 are Private Sector banks. Totally, Public Sector banks have 161 branches and Private Sector Banks have 75 branches. In order to collect primary data for the purpose of the study, Multi Stage Sampling Technique has been adopted.

A sample of six banks (Two Public & Four Private Sector Banks) has been selected at random from the broad categories of banks. Therefore, five branches from each bank have been selected as convenient base. From each branch twenty customers have been selected. Hundred sample respondent from each Banks. Hence, Two hundred Public Sector banks' customers and Four hundred Private Sector banks' customers have been selected. Totally, Six Hundred respondents from Public and Private sector Banks.

6.6.   Data Processing and Analysis

The questionnaire thus filled up was thoroughly checked to ensure accuracy, consistency and completeness. The collected data were scrutinized, edited and tabulated. Regarding the analysis of the data, statistical tools like Chi-square test, Analysis of variance, "Z" test, Factor Analysis, Multiple Regression, Garrett Ranking Techniques and Anova(F-test) were applied. The well known statistical package SPSS 21.0 was employed for analysis purpose.

6.7.   Findings of the Study

The following are the findings of the study:

Progress and Development of Commercial Banks and Brand Management

Origin and developments of Indian banking industry and the overall description of Commercial banks in India. Branding is building a trusting and lasting relationship with consumers; and logos are visual symbols of brand recognition; if the logo, which represents the visual identity of the company, is instantly recognizable by the customer, it signifies that the company has built a brand. "Effective logo must pass through the three stages of conceptualization, Commendation and commercialization. Conceptualization includes seven parameters of Theme, Look, Aesthetics, Complexity, Flexibility, Vulnerability and Memorability. Commendation stage involves appraisal and approval based degree of fit with the image of the company. Commercialization includes launching the logo strategically and innovatively. Precisely, logos should reflect accurately the current identity of the organization, while at the same time be flexible for future development.

With regard to bank brands at the top of the mind among customers, SBI ranked first with the highest score of 2237 out of the selected sample banks. The second and third place goes to CUB and Indian bank with the score of 2156 and 2010 respectively.

It is evident that, in the case of private sector group, CUB ranked first with the highest score of 2156 and ICICI scored 1659 and got second position which clearly brings out the important place and brand power in the minds of customers. In the case of public sector group, SBI and Indian banks hold the first and second ranks.

In the public sector category SBI and Bank of Baroda stood first and second places with score of 1580 and 1573 respectively. In the private sector category, in terms logo identification ICICI bank ranked first with the highest score of 1520 and AXIS bank ranked second with the score of 1505.

It is found that 83.3% of customers got the knowledge about private sector banks through newspapers and in case of public sector banks 75% of the customers got knowledge about bank through bus painting.

It is clear that, in the private sector ICICI bank punch line is most easily identified by customers followed by AXIS bank, HDFC bank and CUB.

In the case of public sector, SBI banks punch line is most easily identified followed by BOB.

It is found that important reason behind banking with the particular bank 'quality' is ranked first with the Garrett's score of 26658 points. It is followed by the reasons 'past experience' ranked second with the score of 22657 points. The third rank is given for the reason 'price' with the score of 22216 points. The reasons 'Rating in consumer report', 'Rating in consumer report' and 'Well known Advertised' is ranked fourth, fifth and sixth with the scores of 20414, 17623 and 12823 points respectively.

Customers' Perception Towards Brand Management in Commercial Banks

The perception level of the customers about their brand management in commercial banks has been examined. In order to examine the perception level, required primary data have been collected by using questionnaire. For which, 21 relevant statements have been given in the questionnaire by using Rensis Likert's 5 point rating scale technique. Such collected data have been analysed with the help of various statistical tools like Standard Deviation, Chi-square, Contingency Co-efficient at 1% level of significance, 'F' test, 'Z' test and Multiple Regression Analysis.

Level of Perception

Private Sector Banks

It is found that the private sector banks majority (41.0%) of the sample customers are having low level perception about their brand management in commercial banks. The mean score is 132.26 and standard deviation is 20.97.

Public Sector Banks

In the case of public sector banks majority (25.0%) of the sample customers are having low level perception about their brand management in commercial banks. The mean score is 129.36 and standard deviation is 21.27.

Age and Perception Level

Private Sector Banks

In age-wise analysis, it is found that private sector banks respondents who are at the age of above 50 years low level perception compared to other age groups.

Public Sector Banks

In the case of public sector banks, higher percentage of respondents who are at the age of 31- 50 years have low level perception compared to other age groups.

Gender and Perception Level

Private Sector Banks and Public Sector Banks

In gender-wise analysis, it is found that private and public sector banks male customers are more than the female customers.

Marital Status and Perception Level

Private Sector Banks

While considering the marital status, it is clear that the average score private sector banks unmarried sample customers is greater than the married sample customers.

Public Sector Banks

In the case of the public sector banks married customers high compared to unmarried sample customers.

Educational Qualification and Perception Level

Private Sector Banks

Regarding the educational level, in the case of private sector 63.3% of the PG & Above, 62.2% of the School level, 61.6% of the UG Level and 60.0% of the No formal education sample customers are having low level perception.

Public Sector Banks

In the case of public sector 80.0% of the PG & Above, 78.8% of the School level, 73.0 % of the UG Level and 52.4% No formal education sample customers are having low perception.

Occupational Status and Perception Level

Private Sector Banks

While examining the occupational status, in the case of private sector 66.4% of the Agricultural, 63.8% of the Student/Housewife, 59.8% Employed, 57.6% of the Business and 57.1 pensioner sample customers are having low level perception.

Public Sector Banks

In the case of public sector 82.5% of the Business, 74.2% of the Agricultural, 70.0% Employed, 69.2% of the pensioner and 57.1 Student/Housewife sample customers are having low level perception.

Annual Income and Perception Level

Private Sector Banks and Public Sector Banks

With regards to annual income, private sector and public sector banks Rs. 2,00,001 to 5,00,000 sample customers are having low level perception about brand management.

Annual Balance and Perception Level

Private Sector Banks and Public Sector Banks

With regards to annual balance, private sector banks 68.5% of the 1Lakh to 3Lakhs and public sector banks, 78.04% of the above 5Lakhs respondents' low perception than the respondents of other groups.

From the inferences of the results of Chi-square test, it is found that the socio-economic characteristics of the sample customers like age, gender, educational level, marital status, occupational status, annual income and annual balance have a no significant association with perception level of the sample customers about their brand management in commercial banks.

In 'F' test, it is found that the association between various socio-economic characteristics like age, gender, educational level, marital status, occupational status, annual income and annual balance of the sample customers and their perception level is found to be insignificant.

From the results of 'Z' test, it can be concluded that there is significant difference in the average scores of gender and marital status (private sector banks) and there is a no significant difference in the average scores of the marital status (public sector banks) and perception level of the sample customers about their brand management in commercial banks.

In Multiple Regression Analysis, it is found that the independent variables explain about 68.2% of the variation in the dependent variable.

Customers' Attitude towards Brand Management in Commercial Banks

To examine the attitude level, necessary primary data are gathered using questionnaire method. For which, 32 relevant statements have been prearranged in the questionnaire by using Rensis Likert's 5 point rating scale technique. Such collected data have been calculated with the help of various statistical tools like Chi-square test, the reliability of statements used to calculate the attitude level has been tested by using Cronbach's Alpha Reliability Analysis. The attitude statements comprised and arranged into a meaningful set using Factor Analysis.

Regarding Chi square test in private sector banks, there is an association between demographic variables viz., Age, Gender, Educational Qualification, Marital Status, Occupation, Annual Income, Total Experience of the respondents and the satisfaction level towards brand management. There is no significant association between Educational Qualification and Total Experience and the satisfaction level towards brand management.

In Public sector banks, the chi square test reveals that there is an association between demographic variables like Age, Gender, Educational Qualification, Marital Status, Occupation, Annual Income, Total Experience of the respondents and the satisfaction level towards brand management. There is no significant association between Occupation and Total Experience and the satisfaction level towards brand management.

From the Cronbach's Alpha reliability test, it is noted that the factors used to examine the attitude level of the sample respondents about the customer are reliable and have an acceptable point of internal consistency.

Principal component analysis was used since the objective is to summarize most of the original information in a minimum number of factors for prediction purpose.

Varimax rotations were used in the study to simplify the factor structure by maximizing the variance of a column of pattern matrix. An Eigen value is the column sum of squares for a factor represents the amount of variance in data. After determination of the common factors, factors scores were estimated for each factor. The common factor themselves were expressed as linear combinations of the observed variables.

In Factor Analysis, 32 statements used to test the attitude level of the sample customer about the scheme have been grouped into 10 factors viz., Brand Association, Brand Performance, Brand Environment, Brand Feeling, Brand Judgment, Brand Image, Brand Quality, Brand Loyalty, Brand Resonance and Brand admirable.

Customers' Satisfaction towards Brand Management in Commercial Banks

Satisfaction of the sample customer towards brand management in commercial bank, necessary primary data are gathered using questionnaires. For which, 19 relevant statements have been prearranged in the questionnaires by using Rensis Likert's 5 point rating scale technique. Such collected data have been calculated with the help of various statistical tools like Chi-square test, 'F' test, 'Z' test, Contingency Co-efficient at 1% level of significance and Cronbach's Alpha Reliability Analysis. The satisfaction statements comprised and arranged into a meaningful set using Factor Analysis. Further, Multiple Regression Analysis has been applied to analyses the influence of various independent variables over satisfaction of the sample customers towards brand management in commercial banks.

It is found that in private sector banks majority (54.8%) of the sample customers are having low level satisfaction among selected commercial bank customers towards brand management. It is found that in public sector banks majority (29%) of the sample customers are having low level satisfaction among selected commercial bank customers towards brand management.

Age and Satisfaction

In age-wise analysis, it is found that in private and public sector banks respondents who are at the age of above 50 years category low level satisfaction compared to other age groups.

Gender and Satisfaction

In gender-wise analysis, it is found that in private and public sector banks male customers are low satisfaction than the female customers.

Marital Status and Satisfaction

While considering the marital status, in the case of private sector sample customers found that 84.4% of the unmarried sample customers and 82.2% of the married sample customers are having low satisfaction. In the case of public sector banks, it is found that 87% of the unmarried and 84.8% married sample customers and are having low level satisfaction about their brand management in banks.

Education Level and Satisfaction

Regarding the educational level, it is found that in both private and public sector banks, the sample respondents belonging to PG and above have low satisfaction followed by other groups.

Occupational Status and Satisfaction

While examine the occupational status, it is evident that in the case of private sector 92.1% of the Student/Housewife have low satisfactory rates followed other sample customers while in case of public sector 92.3% of the pensioner have low satisfactory rates compared to other sample customers.

Annual Income and Satisfaction

In the aspect of annual income, it is found that in the case of private sector & public sector banks, above 5, 00,000 income sample customers are having low level Satisfaction.

From the inferences of the results of Chi-square test, it is found that there is no significant association between the independent variables (age, gender, educational qualification, marital status, occupation and annual income) of the sample towards brand management in commercial banks.

In 'F' test analysis; it is found that the association between various socio-economic characteristics like age, educational qualification, occupational status and annual income of the sample customer and their mean satisfaction level is found to be insignificant.

From 'Z' test analysis, it can be concluded that there is no significant difference in the mean scores of gender and marital status and satisfaction level of selected commercial bank customers towards brand management.

From the Cronbach's Alpha reliability test, it is noted that the factors used to examine the satisfaction level of the sample respondents about the banks are reliable and have an acceptable point of internal consistency.

Principal component analysis was used since the objective is to summarize most of the original information in a minimum number of factors for prediction purpose.

Varimax rotations were used in the study to simplify the factor structure by maximizing the variance of a column of pattern matrix. An Eigen value is the column sum of squares for a factor represents the amount of variance in data. After determination of the common factors, factors scores were estimated for each factor. The common factor themselves were expressed as linear combinations of the observed variables.

In Factor Analysis, 19 statements used to test the satisfaction level of the sample towards brand management in commercial banks have been grouped into 6 factors viz., efficient services, basic services, performance, employee relationship, facilities and bank layout.

Regression analysis is used to examine the relationship between satisfaction score of the customers and independent variables such as gender, age, educational qualification, marital status, occupation, annual income and total experience with this bank.

In this chapter, seven separate regression equation models were worked out to ascertain the influence of different set of independent variables on satisfaction.

The regressions were estimated using cross-section data of 384 private sector and 196 public sector bank sample customers. The results of a regression model were tested   to examine its significance include the R^2; the model F statistic; the individual regression coefficients for each independent variable; their associate 't' statistics; and the individual beta coefficients.

In the case of public sector bank Regression Equation reveals that 0.73% of the total variation in variable Y was explained by seven independent variables ($R^2 = 0.073$). In the case of private sector bank Regression Equation reveals that 1.77% of the total variation in variable Y was explained by seven independent variables ($R^2 = 0.177$). 'F' statistic was calculated to test the significance of R^2. As calculated value of 'F' is greater than the table value, R^2 was significantly greater from zero. It implies that the estimated regression model was significant. Hence, it was concluded that there is a significant relationship between the dependent variable and seven independent variables.

All the seven independent variables were positively associated with dependent variable. The 't' statistic reveals that the coefficients of all the seven variables were statistically significant, implying their relationship was stronger with satisfaction.

6.8.   Suggestions

1. *Reachability towards Logo and Tag Line*

In the present study, while identifying the branding at the top of the minds of the customers, it is found that Bank of Baroda and Axis bank hold the low level of scores (vide table 2.1).

Hence, it is suggested that these two banks have to identify effective Logo & taglines which will be remembered by the customers for ever.

2. *Effective Service through Proper Communication*

In the present study, while analyzing the perception of the customers towards brand management in commercial banks, it is found that 41% of the sample respondents are having Low level of perception in private sector banks and 25% of the sample respondents are having Low level of perception in public sector Banks.

Hence, it is suggested that both private and public sector banks should take all relevant possible steps such as up to date high quality of service, effective communication to customers who are having poor awareness.

3. *Precise Information in Regional Language*

In the present study, while examining the factors influencing the level of attitude of the customers towards Brand Management in commercial banks, it is found that Lack of knowledge of customers regarding banking services is the main factor (Vide table 4.8).

Hence, commercial banks may have to take efforts to enhance the knowledge and awareness about Brand Management in commercial banks through;

- Providing information about various banking services in their regional language.
- Making frequent advertisements in television and newspaper in vernacular language.

4. *Quick and Speedy Service*

In the present study, "Quick and speedy service" is the major factor affecting the satisfaction level of customers about the brand management in commercial banks (Vide table 5.26).

Hence, it is suggested that the commercial banks have to increase the level of customer satisfaction through appointing adequate number of bank staff members, installing automatic customer service kiosks and giving proper training to bank employees.

5. *Problem Solving Skills*

In the present study, it is identified low level of satisfaction due to lack of understanding between bank employees and customers.

Hence, it is suggested that the commercial banks have to inculcate the bank employees about the importance of maintaining cordial relationship with the bank customers.

6. *Employee Relationship towards Customer*

It is found that the main reason behind Low level of customer satisfaction is due to the inattentive attitude of the bank employees towards the customer needs.

Hence, it is suggested that the bank management should insist their employees to give Proper attention to the customers' grievances. By doing so, the brand image of the banks can be enhanced to a greater level.

6.9. General Suggestions

Banking industry became highly competitive due to the entry of private players who provide better services compare to public sector banks. Further due to recession, the NPA's of banks are continuously rising. In this situation it is extremely difficult to retain customers and provide loyalty programmes. Following are some of the suggestion the researcher has suggested:

1. Banks should provide flexi- timing to their customers to improve loyalty.
2. Banks should offer more variety of financial products as per the need of different segments of society.

3. Banks should focus on other service delivery channels such as online banking and ATM which will provide 24x7services to the customers and also reduces the cost to the banks.

4. Banks should provide frequent loyalty programs to the customers, so the customers do not switch over to other banks.

6.10. Suggestions for Further Research

1) The scope of the present study is confined only to Erode district. Therefore, further research can be done on the same basis for banks in other districts.

2) Only six banks have been taken for the study. Further research can be undertaken by taking up more number of banks and respondents to analyse the brand management practices of them.

3) Comparative study of brand management can be carried out in private and public sector banks in Erode district.

6.11. Conclusion

The present study is an attempt to ascertain the brand management in commercial banks: A study in Erode district of Tamil Nadu. The study highlights brand management in selected six banks in Erode district of Tamil Nadu. Thus a good brand management determines customer perception, attitude level and satisfaction. The study will help the Public Sector & Private sector Banks to improve the brand management. It was therefore earnestly hoped that the authorities will consider the suggestions recommended herewith for improving the brand management in Public Sector Banks & Private sector banks.

At this occasion, the commercial banks should remember and follow the famous quote of Mahatma Gandhi;

In this regard, the commercial banks should follow the famous quote of Mahatma Gandhi "A customer is the most important visitor on our premises. He is not dependent on us. We are dependent on him. He is not an interruption in our work. He is the purpose of it. He is not an outsider in our business. He is part of it. We are not doing him a favour by serving him. He is doing us a favour by giving us an opportunity to do so".

BIBLIOGRAPHY

A. Books

1. B. Balaji, Service Marketing and Management, S. Chand & Company Ltd., New Delhi, 2002.

2. Garima Gupta, Marketing of Services- Quality Dimensions, New Century Publications, New Delhi, 2011.

3. Kisholoy Roy, Brand Management(An Indian Perspective), vrinda publications (p) ltd., Delhi, 2012.

4. S.P. Gupta, Statistical Methods, Sultan Chand and Sons, New Delhi, 2000.

5. S.M. Jha, Services Marketing, Himalaya Publishing House, Mumbai, 2000.

6. Prof.(Dr) Ajay Kumar, Brand Management, Wisdom Publications, Delhi, 2012.

7. C.R. Kothari, Research Methodology, Wishva Prakashan Publications, New Delhi, 2002.

8. O.R. Krishnaswami, M. Ranganathan, Methodology of Research in Social Science, Himalaya Publishing House, Mumbai, 2011.

9. Naresh K. Malhotra, Sathyabughan Desh, Marketing Research-An Applied Orientation, Pearson Education, New Delhi, 2009.

B. Journals

1. Randall G. Chapman, Brand performance comparatives, Journal of product and brand management, Vol.2, No.1, 1993.

2. De Chernatony, Dall'Olmo Riley, The chasm between managers' and consumers views of brands: the experts perspective, Journal of strategic marketing, Vol.5, No.2, Pp. 89-104, 1993.

3. De Chernatony, Riley, Modeling the components of the brand, European journal of Marketing, Vol.32, No.11/12, 1998.

4. Fiona Harris, Leslie de chernatony, Corporate branding and corporate brand performance, European Journal of Marketing, Vol.35, Pp. 441-456, 2001.

5. De Chernatony, Segal-Horn Drury, Building a service brand:stages, people & orientations, The service industries journal, Pp. 1-21, 2003.

6. Aron O'cass, Debra grace, Service brands and communication effects, Journal of marketing communications, Vol.10, Pp. 241-254, 2004.

7. Debra Grace, Aron O'cass, Examining the effects of service brand communications on brand evaluation, Journal of product & brand management, Vol.14, Pp.106-116, 2005.

8. Debra grace, O cass, Service branding: consumer verdicts on service brands, Journal of retailing and consumer services, Vol.12, Pp.125-139, 2005.

9. D. Grace, A. O'Cass, Service branding: consumer verdicts on service brands, Journal of Retailing and Consumer Services, Vol.12, No.2, Pp.125-139, 2005.

10. T. W. Aurd, L. Gorchels, T.R. Bishop, Human Resource Management's Role in Internal Branding: An Opportunity for Cross-Functional Brand Message Synergy, The Journal of Product and Brand Management, Vol.14, Pp. 163–169, 2005.

11. Vallaster, de Chernatony, Internal brand building and structuration: the role of leadership, European journal of Marketing, Vol. 40, No. 7/8, Pp. 761-784, 2005.

12. Ram Herstein, Eyal Gamliel, The role of private branding in improving service quality, Managing service quality: An international journal, Vol.16, No.3, 2006.

13. Mosley, Customer experience, organization culture & the employer brand, The journal of product and Brand management, Vol.15, No.2, Pp. 123-134, 2007.

14. O'loughlin Deirdre, Isabelle Szmigin, Services Branding: Revealing The Rhetoric Within Retail Banking, The Service Industries Journal, Vol. 27, No. 4, Pp. 435–452, 2007.

15. Ceridwyn king, Debra grace, Internal branding: Exploring the employee's perspective, Journal of brand management, Vol. 15, Pp. 358-372, 2008.

16. Noel Albert, Dwight Merunka, Pierre Valette-Florence, When consumers love their brands: Exploring the concept and its dimensions, Journal of business research, Vol.61, Pp. 1062-1075, 2008.

17. Mohammad Reza Jalilvand, Arash Shahin, Leila Nasrolahi Vosta, Examining the relationship between branding and customers' attitudes toward banking services: Empirical evidence from Iran", International Journal of Islamic and Middle Eastern Finance and Management, Vol.7, Pp. 214-227, 2008.

18. Margit Raich, Marc-Philipp Crepaz, Fitting new brand principles: First encounter at bank branches, Journal of Brand Management, Vol.16, Pp. 480-491, 2009.

19. Natalie Mizik, Robert Jacobson, Valuing Branded Businesses, Journal of Marketing, Vol. 73, No. 6, Pp. 137-153, 2009.

20. Lars Ohnemus, Is branding creating shareholder wealth for banks?", International journal of bank marketing, Vol.27, No.3, 2009.

21. Robert Hinson, N.Owusu Frimpong, Julius Dasah, Brands and service quality perception, Marketing intelligence & planning, Vol.29, No.3, 2011.

22. Rajeev Batra, Aaron Ahuvia, Richard P.Bagozzi, Brand Love, Journal of Marketing, Vol.76, No.1, Pp. 1-16, 2010.

23. Ceridwyn king, Debra grace, Daniel C funk, Employee brand equity: Scale development and validation", Journal of brand management, Vol.19, Pp. 268-288, 2012.

24. Olokoyo Omowunmi Felicia, Olaleke Oluseye Ogunnaike, Global Economi Meltdown and its Perceived Effects on Branding of Bank Services in Nigeria, Directory of open access journal, Vol.5, No.1, 2012.

25. Joana Cesar Machado, Leonor Vacas-de-Carvalho, Patrício Costa and Paulo Lencastre, Brand mergers: examining consumers' responses to name and logo design, Journal of product and brand management, Vol. 21, No. 6, 2012.

26. Rinalini P Kakati, Smritishikh Choudhury, Measuring Customer-Based Brand Equity Through Brand Building Blocks for Durables, The IUP Journal of brand management, Vol.10, No.2, 2013.

27. Zahra Poorkarimi kokand, Zeinolabedin amini sabegh, Effect of Relationship Marketing on brand loyalty between customers of Bank Refah Kargaran in Tehran city –Iran, IOSR Journal of Business and Management, Vol.14, Pp. 62-66, 2013.

28. Johnson Yeboah, George Dominic Ewur, Evelyn Delali Adigbo, Ernest K. Asirifi, Internal branding in a service industry- A case of banks in Ghana, European scientific journal, Vol.10, No.7, Pp. 218-238, 2014.

29. De Chernatony, Segal-Horn Drury, Building a service brand:stages, people & orientations, The service industries Journal, Pp. 1-21, 2003.

30. Opoku, Robert Ankomah, Nana Atuobi-Yiadom, Cathryn Serwaah Chong, Russell Abratt, The impact of internal marketing on the perception of service quality in retail banking: A Ghanaian case", Journal of Financial Services Marketing, Vol.13, Pp. 317–329, 2008.

31. Anber Abraheem Shlash Mohammad, Shireen Yaseen Mohammad Alhamadani, Service Quality Perspectives and Customer Satisfaction in Commercial Banks Working in Jordan, Middle Eastern Finance and Economics, Pp.60-72, 2011.

32. Abdelghani Echchabi, Hassanuddeen Abd Aziz, Empirical Investigation of Customers' Perception and Adoption Towards Islamic Banking Services in Morocco, Middle-East Journal of Scientific Research, Vol.12, Pp. 849-858, 2012.

33. Sunday Samson Babalola, Perception of financial distress and customers' attitude towards banking, International journal of business and management, Vol.4, No.10, 2009.

34. S. Arun kumar, B. Tamilmani, S. Mahalingam, M. Vanjikovan, Influence of service quality on attitudinal loyaltyin private retail banking: An empirical study, The Journal of management research, Vol.9, No.4, Pp. 21-38, 2010.

35. Mohammad Reza Jalilvand, Farhad Ebrahimabadi, Neda Samiei, The Impact of Branding on Customers' Attitudes toward Banking Services(The Case of Iran's Melli Bank), International Business and Management, Vol. 2, No.1, Pp. 186-197, 2011.

36. R. Johnson, The determinants of service quality: satisfier & dissatisfier, International journal of service industry management, Vol.6, No.5, Pp. 53-71, 1995.

37. Parimal vyas, Measurement of customer satisfaction: A study on banking services, Business perspectives, Vol.4, Pp. 73-87, 2000.

38. S. Shajahan, A study on the level of customer satisfaction on various modes of banking services in india, The ICFAI journal of bank management, Vol.4, 2005.

39. J.K. Mishra, M. Jain, Constituent dimensions of customer satisfaction: A study of nationalized & private banks, Prajnan, Vol.35, Pp. 390-398, 2007.

40. Manoj Kumar Joshi, Customer Services in retail banking in India, ICFAI University Press, Hyderabad, Pp. 59-68, 2008.

41. Komal Sultan Singh, Impact of ATM on customer satisfaction, Business intelligence journal, Vol.2, No.2, Pp. 276-287, 2009.

42. Sandip Ghosh Hazra, Dr. Kailash B.L. Srivastava, Impact of service quality on customer satisfaction, loyality and commitment in the Indian Banking sector, Indian Journal of marketing, West Bengal, 2010.

43. Waqar ul Haq, Bakhtiar Muhammad, Customer Satisfaction: A Comparison of Public and Private Banks Of Pakistan, IOSR Journal of Business and Management, Vol.1, 2012.

44. Mesay sata shanka, Bank Service Quality, Customer Satisfaction and Loyalty in Ethiopian Banking Sector, Journal of Business Administration and Management Science Research, Vol. 1(1), Pp. 001-009, 2012.

45. M.E. Doddaraju, A study on customer satisfaction towards public and private sector banking services, Global Journal of Management and Business Studies, Vol.3,No.3, Pp. 287-294, 2013.

46. Ahmad Jamal, Kamal Nasar, Factors influencing customer satisfaction in the retail banking sector in Pakistan, International journal of commerce and management, Vol.13, No.2, 2013.

C. Reports

1. Annual Report 2016-17, HDFC Bank.

2. Annual Report FY 2017 –ICICI Bank.

3. Performance Review: Quarter ended March 31, 2017.

4. Progress of Banking in India, R.B.I, 2014-15.

D. Websites

1. www.erode.nic.in

2. www.tngov.

3. www.rbi.org.in

4. www.slbc.tn.org.in

5. www.managementstudyguide.com

6. www.stastistics.lared.com

7. www.slideshare.com

8. www.researchgate.net

9. www.sbi.co.in

10. www.planningcommission.nic.in

E. Unpublished Theses

1. R. Shunmughan, Marketing Strategies and Customers Satisfaction in Canara Bank: A Study in Gobichettipalayam Taluk, Erode District, Unpublished Ph.D. thesis submitted to the Bharathiar University, Coimbatore (Supervisor: Dr.E.K.Rayappan), 2007.

2. A. Selvaraj, Cultivation and Marketing of Jasmine in Erode District of Tamil Nadu, Unpublished Ph.D. thesis submitted to the Bharathiar University, Coimbatore (Supervisor: Dr. E.K.Rayappan), 2004.

3. S. Kannusamy, Cultivation and Marketing of Groundnut: A Study with reference to Erode District of Tamil Nadu, Unpublished Ph.D. thesis submitted to the Bharathiar University, Coimbatore (Supervisor: Dr. A.Selvaraj), 2011.

BRAND MANAGEMENT IN COMMERCIAL BANKS: A STUDY IN ERODE DISTRICT OF TAMILNADU

CUSTOMER QUESTIONNAIRE

I Personal Details

1) Name (optional)   :

2) Age   :

3) Gender   :   Male ☐   Female ☐

4) Educational Qualification   :   No Formal Education   ☐
                                                      School Level   ☐
                                                      UG Level   ☐
                                                      PG & Above   ☐

4) Marital Status   :   Married ☐   Unmarried   ☐

5) Main Occupation   :   Business   ☐
                                                      Employed   ☐
                                                      Agriculturist   ☐
                                                      Student & housewife   ☐
                                                      Pensioner   ☐

6) Annual Income (Original)   :   ---------------

7) Your Bank Name   :   AXIS   ☐
                                                      HDFC   ☐
                                                      ICICI   ☐
                                                      CUB   ☐
                                                      BOB   ☐
                                                      SBI   ☐

8) Bank's Branch   :   -------------

9) Types of account(s) maintained in this branch   :   ----------------

10) Average annual balance in your bank a/c

	:	Less than 1Lakh	☐
		1 Lakhs to 3Lakhs	☐
		3Lakhs to 5Lakhs	☐
		Above 5Lakhs	☐
11) Total Experience with this Bank	:	Less than 2 years	☐
		2 -5 years	☐
		Above 5 years	☐

II Brand Details

2.1)   Fill in the below given blanks by the name of banks you know very well

1)________________   2) ________________   3) ________________

4) ________________   5) ________________   6) ________________

7)________________   8) ________________

2.2) Identify the following brand logos of the banks:

1)   ……………………………

2)   ……………………………

3)   …………………………..………

4) CITY UNION BANK LTD   …………………………

5)   ……………………………

6)   …………………………..

2.3)   Where do you find the advertisement of your Bank?

            News paper   ☐
            Magazine   ☐
            T.V   ☐
            Wall painting   ☐
            Hoardings/Banners   ☐
            SMS   ☐
            Bus painting   ☐
            Internet/Web   ☐

2.4)   Kindly the match the bellow given Brand Slogan (Punch Line) with the respective bank brand

No	Bank	Match	No	Punch Line
1	HDFC		A	"Hum Hai Na"
2	ICICI		B	"We Understand Your World"
3	AXIS		C	"Pure Banking Nothing Else"
4	SBI		D	"India's International Bank"
5	BOB		E	Trust & Excellence
6	CUB		F	Everything is the same except the name

2.5)   Which is your most important reason behind banking with this bank? (Give the Ranks)

                                                            Ranks

	Ranks
Personal Recommendation	
Price	
Well Known/Advertised	
past Experience	
Ratings in consumer report	
Quality	

III Perception

Please mark your choice by ticking the appropriate box in each of the statement to reflect your perception/attitude towards your bank's services.

S.No	Statement	SA	A	N	D	SD
1	**Brand Name** The brand name of this bank tells me a lot about what to except from this bank					
	The brand name of this bank tells me a lot about this bank					
	The brand name of this bank means something to me					
	The brand name of this bank sends a message to me about the bank					
	The brand name of this bank tells me everything I need to know about this service					
2	**Price/value for money** This bank's services are reasonably priced					
	This bank offers value for money					
	Using this bank is economical					
3	**Servicesgap** This bank has up-to-date facilities					
	This bank's physical facilities are visually attractive					
	This bank's employees have a neat and well dressed appearance					
	The appearance of the physical facilities of this bank is in keeping with the type of service provided					

S.No	Statement	SA	A	N	D	SD
4	**<u>Core service</u>** The core service provided by this bank suits my needs.					
	The core service provided by this bank is reliable					
	I can depend on this bank to provided good core service					
	This bank provides quality core service					
	The core service provided by this bank is superior					
5	**<u>Employee service</u>** I receive prompt attention from this bank's employees					
	Employees of this bank are always willing to help me					
	The employees of this bank are never too busy to respond to my requests					
	I can trust the employees of this bank					
	Employees of this bank are polite					
	Employees of this bank give me personal attention					
6	**<u>Self image congruence</u>** The image of this bank is consistent with my own self-image					
	Using this bank reflects who I am					
	The kind of person who typically uses this bank is very much like me					

S.No	Statement	SA	A	N	D	SD
7	**Feeling** When using this bank I feel					
	Happy					
	Irritated					
	Good					
	Confident					
	Impressed					
8	**Controlled Communications** Like the advertizing and promotions of this bank					
	I react favorably to the advertizing and promotions of this bank					
	I feel positive toward the advertizing and promotions of this bank					
	The advertizing and promotions of this bank good					
	The advertizing and promotions of this bank do a good job					
	I am happy with the advertizing and promotions of this bank					
9	**Uncontrolled Communications** Publicity about this bank has been significant in affecting my views of this bank					
	Publicity about this bank revealed some things I had not considered about this bank					
	Publicity about this bank provided some different ideas regarding this bank					

S.No	Statement	SA	A	N	D	SD
	Publicity about this bank really helped me formulate my ideas about this bank					
	Publicity about this bank influenced my evaluation of this bank					
	The opinion of my friends/family has been significant in affecting my views of this bank					
	My friends/family mentioned some things I had not considered of this bank					
	My friends/family provided some different ideas regarding this bank					
	My friends/family influenced my evaluation of this bank					

IV Attitude

S.No	Statement	SA	A	N	D	SD
1	**Brand Attitude** Overall I think this bank is very good					
	Overall I think this bank is a nice bank					
	Overall I think this bank is very attractive					
	Overall I think this bank is desirable					
	Overall I think this bank is extremely					
2	**Brand Verdict** I am likely to use this bank in the future					
	I will probably use this bank in the future					
	I will possibly use this bank in the future					
	I have every intention of using this bank in the future					

S.No	Statement	SA	A	N	D	SD
3	I have seriously considered changing my bank					
4	I consider myself to be a loyal customer of this bank					
5	I will switch to a competitor bank that offers more attractive benefits					
6	I will use other products/services offered by this bank in near future					
7	I will switch to a competitor bank when there are problems with this bank's service					
8	I will recommend this bank to others					
9	My bank is					
	Innovative					
	Lack of Knowledge					
	Trust worthy					
	Likeable					
	Admirable					
11	Express your opinion about your bank					
	I can bank with this bank whenever I want					
	I really love my bank					
	I would really miss my bank if it went away					
	My bank is more then a bank to me					
	I really identify with people who bank with this bank					
	I really like to talk about this bank to others					
	I am always interested in learning more about this bank					

S.No	Statement	SA	A	N	D	SD
	I would be interested in learning more about this bank					
	I am proud to have others know, I bank with this bank					
	I like to visit the website of my bank					
	I Compared to other people, follow news about my bank very closely					

V Satisfaction

5.1) Indicate your level of satisfaction /dissatisfaction with each of the following statement ranging from highly satisfied to highly dissatisfied.

S.No	Statement	HS	S	N	DS	HDS
1.	Quick and Speedy Services					
2.	Offering High Quality Services					
3.	Good Care by Financial Advisor					
4.	Wide Range of Products and Services					
5.	Brand/ Image of the Bank					
6.	Price and Fees of Product and Services					
7.	Return on Deposits					
8.	Safety and Security					
9.	Staff Knowledge , Experience and Expertise					
10.	Staff Response					
11.	Better Understanding of customer related problems					
12.	Is Understanding / Knowing the Customer					

13.	Inquiry Counter					
14.	Offer Fun Promotion					
15.	Has Friendly & Courteous Staff					
16.	Banking Hours / Branch Facilities					
17.	Good Hospitailty					
18.	Adequate Parking Facilities					
19.	Physical Appearance					
20.	My bank is Easily Reachable					

Please offer your valuable suggestions to improve the brand management in commercial banks.
